WE CHOSE EACH OTHER

A Mother's Story of Survival, Laughter, and Love
On the North Shore of Lake Superior

By Annie McMillan

All rights reserved. No part of this book may be reproduced or transmitted in any form or by any means, electronic or mechanical, including photocopying, recording, or by any information storage and retrieval system, without permission from the copyright owner.

This book was printed in the United States of America.

Copyright © 2023 Annie McMillan

ISBN: 9798858551768

DEDICATION

For William and Molly without whom I doubt I would be alive to tell this story.

With special gratitude to Molly who unknowingly named my book when she recently phoned to say, "I was talking to William, and you know, Mom, we each went through our own hell at different times, in different ways, as children, as young adults, and even now as we continue to grow. We were shattered at one point but look at us now!! We made it! And that is because at the heart of it all, we chose each other."

In honor of the McMillans; my parents especially. Thank you, God, for blessing me. I am so fortunate to have been raised in this family.

I knew as I was writing that I wanted to dedicate this book to my children, my parents, my AA and my Alanon families. Within those relationships I learned to survive, live and experience love. What I didn't know was how humbling it would be to describe it all. So, I begin by asking that you accept me as a slow learner.

I am aware of my many mistakes, my self-centered decisions, my naivete, my promises and my bull-headed assumptions that I knew what was right.

I know that now. I understand.

Thank you for sticking with me and helping me. I found my Higher Power. I did the best I could. I see now that with practice we were all able to find lives of usefulness and joy.

Thank you for the sheer delight of being your mother, your grandmother, your daughter, your sister, your wife, your fellow traveler.

I am sorry.

I am grateful.
My heart is full.

I love you,

Annie

TABLE OF CONTENTS

Introduction	1
Chapter 1 Climbing	5
Chapter 2 The Box Mountain	8
Chapter 3 The Birthday Party	26
Chapter 4 Lists	31
Chapter 5 Hello Two Harbors	36
Chapter 6 My New Home Meeting	43
Chapter 7 80% of Life is Showing Up	45
Chapter 8 The Affair	60
Chapter 9 A Day at a Time	72
Chapter 10 Seagull Friends	82
Chapter 11 An Angel Named Christine	86
Chapter 12 The Wizard of Oz	95
Chapter 13 Sex	101
Chapter 14 Where It All Began	111
Chapter 15 Cocoa – Another Angel	121
Chapter 16 Angus	134
Chapter 17 Pet Story – The Next Generation	143
Chapter 18 The Times They Are A Changing	158
Chapter 19 Lake County Jail	165
Chapter 20 Rhoda	178
Chapter 21 More Jail and Sean	185
Chapter 22 The Journey Within The Journey	206
Chapter 23 Good Night	231

Introduction

Here's the good news.

There is a path. You will be able to follow it. It is more than interesting, and it will take you places you never thought you'd go or certainly like. The path is actually quite humorous; no, downright, laugh-out-loud funny once you decide that survival requires you to toss out all protocol, all expectations of appropriate choices, and all normal operating procedures. Instead you will be picking up and honing some new tools called ingenuity, tenacity, passion for a great life in the face of shattering circumstances, and attitude. *Nothing* will stop you from seeking and finding joy, delight in each day and a ferocious, get-out-of-my-way desire to master what you need to learn in order to survive.

You will hate being crummy at how to do the Food Shelf, for example, and will develop an insatiable appetite for excelling at how to provide for yourself and your children when you have nothing.

You will compete like an Olympian with those mystery mothers who figured out how to beat you to the best pair of boots for your five-year-old, at Neighbor to Neighbor or Goodwill.

You will become a great playmate. You will have fun every day. You won't believe the adventures you can have in a 24-hour period, day after day.

You will perfect the skill of the long-term shuffle and the short-term scramble, dances you will effortlessly slip into as you handle the crisis-du-jour, which 90% of the time is financial.

You will make so many mistakes. I mean, absolute showstoppers that cause your tragedy and ruin to sink well past the point of no return. What's worse, you'll make those same mistakes quite a few times, which will blow your mind.

However, you will also experience some equally unbelievable moments of brilliance and good fortune when you will slap your side and do the endzone spike with an affirmative, "Yay-us!" as if to say to the universe, "Bring it on, I'm getting somewhere!"

Now here's the bad news.

This path; it doesn't lay itself out ahead of you so that you can actually see it. There is no map. There are no Cliff notes, no how-to manual, no <u>Survival for Dummies</u> that tell you how to do this thing called, "My husband just left with another woman. I am 52 years old with two young children, one a toddler. I am fighting off bankruptcy. I'm crazy with menopause. I am broke, I need a job. I just moved here last week and live seven miles out of town in a cabin in the woods. It is just me and my two kids. And the tool kit that comes with 50 plus years of Boomer living just doesn't seem all that useful at the moment."

I had answered the phone and heard, "Hi, Ann. Jack. I'm not coming up."

"Oh, hi, honey. You mean this weekend? How much longer do you think you'll need to tie things up?"

"I'm not coming up."

"Well, that's okay. William and Molly really miss you." As well they should have. Our children adored their dad. William, eight years old, was his father's righthand dude. They were inseparable in their endless pursuit of increasingly more difficult karate belts. Both introverts and voracious readers, they hung together Saturday mornings running errands in Jack's fire engine red truck, so they could spend the rest of their weekends playing video games and reading Harry Potter.

Molly, three years old, was her daddy's princess, well aware that she occupied that treasured place in the eyes of her father. By default Molly and I were the other pair in the family and happily so. But when it came to cuddling, Molly was the one that fit perfectly into Jack's lap, while William and I found our spots around the edges.

"Well, we can keep ourselves busy unpacking. Lord knows we've got boxes; and I know this sort of thing always takes longer than you think. When shall we look for you?"

"I'm not coming up."

"You mean …at all?"

"Yeah."

"What does that mean?"

"I found someone else."

"Like another woman? Oh. Oh, my God."

You hold your stomach and drop the phone moving quickly to find a place to lie down before you fly apart and spill all over. You curl into a half-moon on the sort of made bed that represents your best efforts at settling in over the past four days. Your eyes are stuck at wide open and filling with tears, "Oh no, oh no, oh no." Everything is dark and still until, "Mama are you crying?"

And then, by some miracle you snap out of it and hear yourself uttering the first of a thousand great responses to the shattering brokenness, "Yes, Molly, I am. But I can do that later. Come on. Let's go climb those boxes in the garage and see what we can find."

And you do. And you do. And you do until through sheer determination and refusing to give up, the grace of God surrounds you with angels disguised as people, blessings disguised as serendipity, and you make it. You really make it and the picture looks pretty good! You look good. You are upright. The kids look good; they are thriving. You are working. Your car is more than decent. You have a bank account that, granted, hovers too close to zero too many days, but you are covering your expenses. Best of all, you are happy and moving on.

      If you are in a place where you hardly know where to begin because everything is crumbling so fast you can't possibly catch the pieces, just know that you will be alright. You will be alright. In fact, you are alright in the most important ways. It just won't seem like it for a while. Suit up. Show up. What have you got to lose? Honestly. When you are at the end of your rope, who cares anymore about what was supposed to be or what you were supposed to become? Let it go and get out there. Get your game face on because there is your life to be lived. You are it now. You are the provider for your children who, I can guarantee you, will want to eat in a few hours and who will be looking to you for everything, to provide for them, to love them. You can do it. I know you can do it − and here are some stories to carry with you so you know you are not alone.

Chapter 1
Climbing

I climb. I like going up. I like to look out and I like to look far and wide. My body swells when I am up high and on top of the world, whatever little piece of the world I am on. I feel better. I believe in goodness, and I know hope.

If, by magic, you captured me and confined me to a small space, I wouldn't burrow, or hug my arms around me so that I could close my eyes and journey into the recesses of my mind; oh, no; I would reach up and find the closest thing to pull myself up and I would climb.

I can see that I have been oriented in this way for a long, long time; and I expect that I arrived at birth with basic wiring so that climbing makes sense to me.

I climbed Kilimanjaro.

I climbed the rocky cliffs of Lake Superior.

I have climbed those indoor rock-climbing walls at the Mall of America and REI.

I climbed Mount Washington.

I always climb the slippery, steep embankment on hikes along the North Star Association River to get to the trails on top, which is so much more interesting than taking the gradual walk up the available groomed path.

I love the wind, too.

And I like to race.

I like to race and win, but I still like the race if I have run as fast as I can.

I love speed - not excessive speed but I like moving more than I like sitting. I walk fast. I have never ambled. If I am sad, I walk fast more slowly.

I would rather know my surroundings by picking up, tossing, molding, pushing or pulling than by looking and assessing.

I thank God for his handiwork; that he created me predisposed to move... really move, because moving it out was what we needed. He put in my path seemingly unrelated people and events, at just the right times that became lynchpins for the formula we needed in order to survive. They sparkled so I wouldn't miss them when I reached to gather them and bring them along for the climb.

Before the mountain ever came into view, I was given something for my spiritual amulet - a conversation with the counselor at Lutheran Brotherhood who reacted to my fear of not having anything - money, my home, my former standard of living.

"You know, Annie, I have a lot of moms who come to see me every day that have not had the education and the opportunities that you have. They have a lot less to work with and they have figured out how to put food on the table, dress their children in designer clothes, send them off to school with brand new back-packs full of brand-new school supplies, and with new winter boots and snowsuits when the first snowfall hits," she began.

"You would never be able to pick out the kids of those moms. They look like everybody else or better." she continued, looking me straight in the eye.

"Do you know how those moms do it?" she asked without waiting for a reply I didn't have, "Those moms have skills that you don't have. They are masters at a system that can provide for them and their kids. They know *everything* about how the system works, where to be and when to be there. They know the right places, the right days and the right lines to be in to make sure they get first crack at the cream of the crop."

That's all I needed to hear. Lynn didn't need to add her closing comment, "You will have to apply yourself and learn about a whole world that is foreign to you. You can succeed at this, too. You suck at it right now, but it can be learned and there are champions. GO!"

It would seem that there would be notable differences between climbing a mountain and suddenly figuring out how to survive without a husband and an income when you are facing an impending bankruptcy and divorce. At first blush, climbing a mountain could seem rather simple: put one foot in front of the other and go up. Surviving? complicated: think of every area needing attention, do research, anticipate problems and solutions, prioritize before you can even take a step.

No. Not to me. They were the same. Both had overwhelming goals: Stand on Top of the Mountain *or* Be Financially Independent with Happy Children. Both required taking steps on a path to the next way marker: Go 3/4 of a mile up the path at a 30-degree pitch, using hand-over-hand climbing as needed *or* Meet with the social worker at Lake County Social Services, referencing mitts-full of bills and abusive correspondence to make my points as needed. I saw them as the same.

Without being ridiculous about the analogy, loving climbing and understanding that I was at the base of a very tall and rugged mountain worked for me. I wanted to climb. I was born to climb. I knew I could climb, and I could count on that. I was all I needed in the most important and basic place. Deep in my heart, I had no doubts. I knew I was meant for this.

Now if I could just remember that.

Chapter 2
The Box Mountain

The afternoon of the same Saturday that Jack said he wasn't coming... at all... I rallied and called for help. Actually, I don't think I was calling for help. It just seemed that I should telephone someone and tell them what happened. The person I thought to call was Tom, the minister who married us. Tom was young and handsome and fun and a great youth minister at St. Paul's oldest and most beautiful Presbyterian church where I had grown up, infant to adult, in the tradition of a close and committed Christian family. As a grandchild of George and Lillian Hart, pillars of the church, and the eldest daughter of Robert McMillan, Jr. and Elizabeth McMillan, I was immersed in Sunday school, music, choir, youth leadership, and the values of service, humility and gratitude.

Tom was a good friend; the perfect minister to marry Jack and me on the day after Christmas 18 months earlier. It was my second marriage; for Jack, too, after living together for ten years. Being in a blended family with seven children including our own two helped me find a place in the past for my divorce from my first husband. I had been married to Josh, my high school sweetheart, for twenty years in the one and only marriage I ever expected to have. Despite alcoholism, well, really because of alcoholism and bulimia, I had found my way to treatment and a life of recovery; so, although our marriage had difficulties, I had been happy as a young mother of two sons, and the wife of my only true love. When things inevitably fell apart it took a long time for my broken heart to heal enough to fall in love again.

On December 26th, the night Tom married Jack and me, that heartbreak was far, far away. Seasonal evergreen trees and boughs, wreaths, poinsettias and holly adorned House of Hope Presbyterian church and filled the air with the aromas of Christmas – my favorite season of the year, my favorite holiday, my wedding in a most magical time and place. I chose to process by myself down the long, candlelit aisle, meeting my two older sons, Oliver and Christopher, at the altar. My dress was elegant, white satin and silk, with a fitted bodice and scoop neck, sleeveless with narrow straps and a narrow skirt that fit my body all the way to the floor. Little satin buttons went all the way down the back and my favorite part, a short train became a bustle for the reception. I wore a veil that my oldest son sent flying when his muscular right arm came in a little too high to link with mine. After a slightly audible gasp and muffled, "Sorry Mom," plus a variety of hands working to set it back in the middle of my head, we went on. The boys gave me away and we proceeded to enjoy a grand and beautiful evening wedding. Teenage pouting and the late arrival of the soloist were easily outshined by our beautiful children who were spit-shined and gussied up in bridesmaid, flower girl, or groomsman garb, having the time of their lives as we drove in a white limo from the church to the University Club to dine and dance the night away with our guests.

When Tom answered the phone, I blurted out, "Jack left with another woman." And through the tears added, "I just really want to be home in my own church right now with the people who love us."

To Tom's question, "Can you do that?" I answered, "No."

"Will you pray for us, I mean keep us in your prayers?" I squeaked.

"I already am," I heard Tom say; and then, after a long silence and more tears, we both said, "Good-bye."

I remember being very clear in my head that we could go back to the Twin Cities but no, we wouldn't. Leave and go home? That didn't work for me. This was our home now and we were already into our new life, with or without Jack. Even though the children and I had just arrived, there was security in the dream of living in the cabin, our heavenly retreat, our family's favorite place in the world that sat high upon the rocky hills overlooking Lake Superior. I bought it to be lived in and now we were here.

It was magical how the cabin became ours in the first place. The year before I bought it, Jack and I were vacationing on Seven Mile Beach in the Cayman Islands. I told him about Shakti Gawain's book, <u>Creative Visualization</u>, and specifically, the pink bubble technique of holding your dream in your mind and then releasing it into the universe in an imaginary pink bubble. I believed in karma and in attracting energy that could fulfill dreams. I understood my imagination and passion for ideas as God given, deserving of my attention and worthy of pursuit when unexpected opportunities presented themselves. So, after Jack and I toured a beautiful home on the beach that was for sale, we took a walk imagining a retreat where our family and friends could join us…a perfect pink bubble moment. The sand was warm as we sat in the shallow water and raised our arms to the sky after visualizing our individual dreams which I imagined ascending in two imaginary pink bubbles becoming a part of the western Caribbean sky.

When we returned from our trip, months passed without either of us ever mentioning that afternoon. And then one day I received a letter notifying the membership of the North Star Association that a cabin was for sale. The sale of a cabin was a rare occurrence. It was expected that families would pass their cabins down to the next generations who would step up to care for the land and the structures as their part in carrying on the legacy of a magical place to summer and winter in Northern Minnesota.

There were only 50 cabins in this exclusive association. My stepfather owned two, right next to each other; and I think because I was an adult child on some expanded family list, I also received the announcement in the mail. When I read the letter, I called right away to see if it was still available. When

I explained who I was and my relationship with the association, the owners invited us to drive up at our convenience and stay a couple of nights. That very weekend, Jack, our baby, William, and I drove up to the North Shore, found the key, and opened the front door which looked out floor to ceiling glass windows. There before us was a breathtaking 180-degree view of Lake Superior. At the same moment, Jack and I looked at each other and said, "The pink bubble."

And it was. As magically as it appeared, it became ours. Financing, ownership approval and the logistics of purchasing went quickly and smoothly. The cabin itself was less than 5 years old, cedar and glass, in perfect condition all by itself surrounded by the north woods, its furry inhabitants and walking/cross country trails. The architect himself said it was his favorite of all the houses he had built up and down the shore. Perfect in her Biblical cross shape, with 30-foot ceilings, it was designed so that the horizontal beams in the great room required no additional hardware to support the roof and keep the cabin standing. There was a floor to ceiling fireplace made from boulders along the shore, a "swing bed" room that had three all glass walls where a double bed hung by chains from the cedar plank ceiling. Other necessary spaces included a bathroom and a half, a galley kitchen, an oversized single garage and a carpeted loft full of futons accessible only by the eight-step ladder that went straight up - no railing. Sprinkle in some living room couches, chairs, and a long dining room table. Add a pantry, a teensy laundry room, and a deck off the back that overlooked the Lake, the woods, and the island offshore, and there stood our pink bubble dreams. Our cabin was a jewel and now William, Molly and I were calling it home.

More tears, more wiping them away, more blowing my nose and then out to the garage because that's where the box mountain was and that's where there was something that we could all do.

The box mountain was a solid mass of different sized cardboard boxes, expertly loaded onto the moving truck by Jack at our home in St. Paul, then U-hauled by the children and me to the cabin in Two Harbors. Once unloaded, the boxes filled our oversized, single stall garage wall to wall and floor to nearly ceiling, which presented a puzzle since the cabin was already beautifully furnished and very comfortable. The sheer size and presence of the box mountain indicated that I must have thought that permanently moving in required bringing more stuff, a lot more stuff. Unfortunately, the time for me to say to myself, "Not necessarily so," had passed. Stuff was on the premises, and we had to figure out what exactly was in those boxes and where were we going to put it.

There was enough room between the boxes on the top and the garage rafters for William to be able to stand up. Molly had free reign at ground level where a two-foot walkway surrounded the boxes. For me the box mountain was an introduction to the first of many disguised blessings - a must-take-action priority so in my face it was if the mountain spoke to me directly, "Come do something with me or you'll never get moved in!" As such it displaced the terror of the morning's news and I responded with behavior that answered, "Okay! I got it."

I summoned my expert climber. "William, how would you like to see if we can tackle the box mountain in the garage? I need someone to climb to the top."

"Sure, I'll do it," William said as he came running to meet Molly and me who were already looking toward the summit.

"Okay, William," I began, "your job is to climb to the top and open a box. Then look inside and tell me what you see, and I will tell you to send it down or close it up. If it is too heavy, I'll come up and we'll figure out how to get it down together. Got it?"

"Yup," I heard as William scrambled to find a path up.

"Molly, you stay down here with Mom. Here are some crayons for you to color the boxes and maybe later we can climb up together. Okay?"

"Yup!" Molly answered, proud to be following her brother's lead.

The children looked forward to time on the box mountain, thank God; it was what we needed in addition to what we needed to do. So, we spent part of every day all June moving stuff here and there, creating an even more comfortable home and, more importantly, a storage catacomb underneath the house where there was 1,000 square feet of dry space the size of our main floor. This ground floor, or more correctly this below ground floor, was solid rock and dirt, more rolling than flat, and roughly covered with two large pieces of thick plastic that offered up an abundant crop of dead and alive mice; hence, its new name, the Mouse House.

Getting stuff to the Mouse House from the garage which was at true ground level, was a workout in itself, requiring a steep descent down a ten step, wooden ladder with no railings, only accessible through a thirty-pound trap door in the floor of the pantry. Once down the ladder, those who dared to go on, walked side-ways to a smaller ladder at the end of a long wall of cinderblocks, where if you were a Hobbit you could climb up and walk right in.

Oh! Did I forget to mention the Mouse House ceiling height was three feet...except where the duct work dropped it to two? Even Molly had to bend down a little to walk around. William avoided entering altogether and I crawled on my hands and knees or squatted - butt to the floor in order to waddle like a duck. Dragging stuff to plastic storage containers, stacking them where possible and cleaning as I went was an exhausting and painful exercise as if some weird physical torture had been designed to out-hurt my emotional wounds.

I say we tackled the box mountain by day because by night I came face to face with information buried deep inside the box mountain, another unexpected blessing not without its own excruciating pain, but with some answers to the questions about betrayal whirling inside and all around me. "What happened?" "How could this have happened?" "Why did this happen to me?" "What is happening?"

In the box marked "Bedside Journals", I came upon all of Jack's journals in addition to my own, together with other things I had packed from our bedroom. We had each made use of one of a pair of elegant 18th century Italian bedside tables to hold our journals, pens, inspirational books, Carmex, flashlights, love notes and other personal trinkets. Having had nearly 40 years between the two of us in 12 step programs, we were well acquainted with the value of journaling. It was common for each of us to be in bed at night writing our own end-of-the-day thoughts. It was also completely understood that journals were private.

Funny though, when I opened that box and saw Jack's journals, I thought differently. I hesitated, thinking for the first time that I might have a right to read them. It was ten at night, cool to cold, the way it gets on summer nights on the north shore of Lake Superior, and I was beginning to feel the chill sitting on the cold cement step in the garage in khaki shorts, a sweatshirt and tennies. "What's in there?" I heard myself whisper, holding the journal that was on top of the pile. It was a tan, 8 & 1/2 x 11 spiral bound, wide lined notebook, the kind you would take on a science field trip for insect notes.

"I'll feel terrible if I read this," I thought to myself, *"and I don't need to add a pile of guilt to this mess. On the other hand, who the hell cares? You left! If you don't want someone else reading your thoughts, then take your shit with you. My AA sponsor would say, 'Don't read other peoples' journals.'"*

I sat a moment longer and then opened to the first page where I began reading an eight-year-old entry dated 10/23/93. What started out referencing an Indian summer day at the cabin with the wind blowing from the south, quickly turned into a pornographic, explicit description of a violent assault on a woman viewed at close range and in slow motion - sodomy, and how that related to Jack's masturbating, spelled masterbating. Following were a few more rambling sentences on fantasies and real-life frustrations with enemas and anal masturbation, a paragraph of reflection on what worked and what common household items required more exploration. Then, as if it flowed naturally and seamlessly, Jack concluded with a return to the topic of family adding it was a "guys weekend" with our two-year-old son, William. Lest the reader think this was an all play and no work get-away, Jack added that he was putting up a chandelier in the cabin and that the leaves were gone.

I was numb.

I stayed still and breathed shallow breaths quietly, only slightly moving my eyes from left to right to left. Finally, I looked up from the page because I had to go to the bathroom. Walking into the room about which I had just read, sitting on the toilet close enough to touch the bathtub was not the same routine activity that used to occur for me without much thought many times a day. I saw everything in a new way - and not a nice way. I no longer looked with innocence at shampoo bottles and the back scratcher that sat in the shower caddy. As I walked slowly through my cabin back to the garage, my home transformed itself into a pornographic "I SPY" game - "Can you find three things on shelves that look common and do something very uncommon?" It didn't take much imagination after reading Jack's vivid description of his future agenda, sexually, for me to see that some of my most treasured art and pieces of sculpture could have dual utility. For days I couldn't shake it; a paradigm shifted and there was no going back.

The journal entry itself was a grammatical disaster and particularly annoying in its frequent misspelling of the word masturbate. I couldn't help but notice. Obviously, this was a chilling look at a man I didn't recall meeting, befriending and certainly marrying. I was shaking. I was afraid for me and the children. The 17 other, different colored, 8 & 1/2 x 11 journals sat there in a pile, dated, each one completely filled as far as I could tell. I no longer cared about journal etiquette and quickly put them in chronological order beginning with the year 1987. I read until five in the morning when I realized I was shivering, and that my right cheek had fallen asleep from sitting in one position for so long.

Unbelievable. From 1987 to 1998 Jack had journaled almost every morning and night, or sometimes just night, recording his life as a victim. I was reading the story of our life, where I was referenced in most entries by name but characterized and described as prey. I was reading the story of a man whose string of thwarted plans, schemes and unrealized dreams were the fault of everyone else. When his path originally crossed with mine, he saw me as a woman who had the potential to deliver for him. Therefore, I was worth grooming as long as I didn't catch on.

I read every night from the time I put the children to bed until one or two in the morning. My days and nights were separate lives. The children and I climbed the box mountain by day and in the strangest way I would climb again at night, this time into bed, leaning against propped up pillows, surrounded by blankets and quilts to keep me warm when the cool of the night settled in. As if I had a great novel in my hands, I would hold the next red or green or blue notebook and gently open to a new page.

Once I was over the initial shock of what I was reading, I became engrossed in the story; the day-by-day, raw, inner workings of a mentally ill person. The profanity and pornography lost their shock power, desensitizing me to passages I found I simply "read through" as I adjusted to Jack's world at the same time I detached from him as my husband. I was fascinated, curious, intrigued with what was unfolding, hardly able to wait for the day to end so I could read some more. Without deliberation or intention on my part, the story drew me in and moved me. I mean literally moved me emotionally through disbelief, past disgust, toward compassion until I settled into a final state of understanding and sadness. What a colossal waste of a human life.

I had discovered that Jack was a predator, introduced as a young boy to sexual abuse in his family. I knew about his past. He had carefully disclosed as much as I would tolerate when we were dating, always taking me just past the point where I wouldn't listen anymore, but further than I had been before in terms of knowing, then accepting who he was and what he wanted from me. In the beginning I listened, tolerating more and more of his escapades and fantasies, mere steppingstones to his goal which was to be a willing partner in whatever he wanted from me sexually.

"Annie, there is something that I haven't told you that is hard for me to talk about, but I want to be honest with you," Jack said as we pulled up to the Guthrie theater in our second year of dating. I had season tickets, my favorite hold over from my marriage to Josh, and there was nothing I loved more than dressing for the evening and going to the theater. We arrived in plenty of time to take in one of Shakespeare's classics. I had driven because Jack only had a motorcycle . We were about to get out of the car I had expertly parked for a bonus view of the sun setting over the Walker Art Center's sculpture garden.

"Oh. What is it?" I asked, wary of what I was going to hear. I was familiar with this opening. I had been there before for many other disclosures: his two divorces, his bankruptcy, his sex addiction, his penniless status, his lack of employment. And yet I was still there. He always brought me back from my initial reaction which was, "I'm sorry, Jack. You know how much I love being with you, but this just isn't going to work for me. I don't think we really have a future."

Silence.

I would add, "I need some space."

Jack would calmly respond with, "Of course. I cannot expect you to stick around, sweetness."

We would part ways with a string of just-end-it banter,

"I'm sorry."

"Ya me too."

"I just had to be honest even though it might be the end"

"Ya, me too. Well, good-bye."

"Good-bye."

One to two weeks would pass during which Jack would send flowers, notes of gratitude for blessing his life, and corny cards about how sexy hot I was. Sometimes he would just show up and put those great hands of his on my lower back until the seduction ended in bed. He was a slow kisser, a great lover and sure enough we would be back together again. I never said, "No."

That was the pattern he introduced. I learned my part which was to rationalize my fears and to repeat the dance until his world replaced mine. Over time we stayed more and more to ourselves. We spent hundreds of thousands of dollars of my money on cars, food, trips to Hawaii and the Cayman Islands, skiing in Lake Tahoe, new John Deere tractors, expensive tools, a treehouse and zipline, vacation homes, his business, his clothes, all mixed together with plenty of fun, attention and appreciation for me.

Jack was a big kid, all in for anything fun, especially if it made me happy. I think he actually loved my ideas because they were fun for him, fun for our kids, and usually involved building something at his Craftsman workbench with his complete set of Craftsman tools; a Friday Night Date purchase I had popped for the night we walked around the Mall of America.

Four years into our relationship Jack had moved in with me and was well aware of my love of winter. When the lake in back of our house froze for the first time each year, usually around Thanksgiving, it was no secret that I had a happy heart. On this particular evening I must have been quiet but exuding some good energy because Jack said, " I can see you are excited that the lake froze today. It's a new winter! What are you thinking?"

Who doesn't love that romantic moment when your prince asks you what is in your heart of hearts like he can deliver anything? Which in Jack's case was true because he knew I would pay for it.

I asked, "What would it take to plow a big, I mean really big, ice rink off the dock, with hockey nets, lights strung up in the trees or mounted out on the ice; with music over a sound system so we could have a big winter wonderland party with our friends and families and the children's school friends and families - the kind of party that could start in the afternoon with sledding, cross country skiing, broomball and go into the night with a bonfire and hot chocolate outside if people wanted to skate under the stars? It's what I've always wanted, our kitchen full of food for making sandwiches, crockpots with soups and chili, hot cider on the stove, a fire in both fireplaces, caroling at the piano and happiness - lots of happiness."

As soon as the ice was thick enough to support skaters and a plow, my dream came true. Our plow (one piece of the full-attachment-package that I had purchased along with a new John Deere tractor on a date night Jack had arranged at the Northern Store) was now in Jack's hands. Jack got his new toy, and I got my wish.

It was all there with an unexpected surprise - a wide path plowed along the shore of the whole lake so we could pair skate to Kenny G's Classic

Christmas Album! Looking down from our picture window in the house onto the lake where twinkling lights lit up the trees and flood lights dressed the rink; I easily dismissed the party which never happened. I was completely happy in the private moments on our pond, pair skating with Jack on crisp, cold nights when the moon was out, and the stars were bright. Kenny G played into the still darkness accompanied by the rhythmic sound of our gliding skates as they cut into the ice - first right, then left, then right, then left. Fluent in my love language, Jack would stand across from me, take both my hands making an x in front of our bodies, turn us to face in the Same direction and whoosh! we would circle the lake until we were winded.

There is nothing as sweet as a warm kiss in the winter cold, hugging and being hugged by the bundle of layers and winter jackets of the person you are kissing.

Jack knew what made me happy: to hangout as a family, to sweep me off my feet, to cook, to make love by the fire, to walk in the woods and have our own 12 step meeting. Big picture, Jack controlled what once was my expansive life, successfully whittling it down to an existence that was narrow and small. He kept me happy, and I accepted him. I was only too happy to shower him with everything he wanted.

In the thirteen years Jack and I were an item, the compilation of his disclosures produced what I believe was a full picture of his life, past and present. His father raped him, his grandfather belittled him and beat him up while his mother, an alcoholic, was unable to protect her son. The Stewarts were poor, there was nothing in school to keep Jack there, so he hit the streets at 16 and learned to leverage his good looks, sexuality, and intuition about people. When we met at an AA meeting, he was 32, smooth with just the right blend of quiet mystery, flirtation and seductive helplessness, looking for some companionship while he was raising his three children under the age of seven.

"It's my first week on the job since my wife walked out with another man," I heard him say.

I bit.

So, two years later in front of the Guthrie he said, "I go to the movies on Hennepin every morning."

Silence.

"Annie, do you know what that means?" Jack continued.

"No," I replied. "I mean, I know there is the Orpheum theater and I have been to a lot of live, black box theater in the arts district."

"It's not that kind of theater. It's porn."

"I don't know what you are talking about," was all I could come up with. I was starting to sweat.

"Well, it's part of the adult bookstore. You go in, you pay, and then you go to one of the small booths with a chair - in a big dark room - and then you watch by yourself and masturbate while you are watching porn films."

There was something resembling enjoyment in Jack's demeanor when he told me, speaking slightly more slowly and articulating each point. I didn't like it.

I responded, "Oh. I don't think I want to know anymore."

"I'm trying to quit and I am talking about it at SAA (Sex Addicts Anonymous), but I went this morning and I feel so dirty, so disgusted with myself. I couldn't help it… but keeping it from you just makes the secret worse."

Good God, what a way to step out for an evening at the theater. I just wish I had been able to find words, to speak for myself.

"Stop! Zip it. I honestly don't care how dirty you feel. Talk to your sponsor, call someone, anyone! Anyone but me! I do not want to know. Not here, not now. This is not the time or place and furthermore, I don't want to do this anymore! Bu-bye now."

But I had no idea what to do with Jack's admission.. I didn't think I should judge. What did I know? I hadn't walked in his shoes. I had done plenty of disappointing things in my life like lying to my mom in second grade about staying home from school when I really wasn't sick. I had lousy boundaries and clearly no perspective. I was in over my head, so I offered up,

"I'm sorry, Jack, I don't know what to say except …'No thank you?' … This just isn't for me, but I'm glad you are getting help." And then after a pause, "Shall we go in? We might as well go to the play since we're here."

Shakespeare plays are long, but that was one long evening, followed by the usual break-up dance. We were two years in - and I stayed for another eleven.

I know now that I continued to play right into Jack's hands because there was something there for me. I was willing to be his prey, to believe his compliments, to bring no discretion to our excessive spending and expensive lifestyle. I preferred to be "loved" rather than to find a way to love myself and start again after the end of my first marriage of 21 years to my high school sweetheart. My dreams had gone up in smoke and my heart was still broken when I met Jack. I didn't want to do the work, to heal, to be okay with me on my own, not when I could be swept off my feet and run away.

All of that became clear over time, but when I first read Jack's journals, I wasn't thinking about taking responsibility for myself or trying to make sense out of my own life. I was simply reading his intimate story… his heart of hearts… no, his accounting of his personal scheme that had been skillfully kept a secret in the 13 years we were together. I was reading a story in which Jack was conning me, a story in which Jack was curiously in awe of me, maybe in love with me, but mostly invested in masterfully conning me, his prey, to provide the lifestyle, its comforts and toys he believed he deserved. Scary, especially when I began to snap out of it. In the middle of many nights when I finished reading, I allowed reality to surface: I was also reading about my life or more accurately, Jack's life in which I played a part.

"I guess if you are going to be conned, you can take some pride in knowing it was by one of the best," said my therapist who added, "He sounds very good." Thankfully God put me in her care. She was a highly respected psychologist at the University of Minnesota in Duluth who ran a men's therapy group for sex addicts in addition to teaching and working in her family practice. She taught me to see it all differently. Prior to meeting Jack I never thought of a con artist as a bona fide profession. In fact, I never ever thought of anything related to a con artist. But I started to see it now. It was his primary activity. It not only paid the bills, it eliminated them altogether while he posed as a karate teacher in a business that did little more than break even.

Jack did extremely well for himself. In the first few months we dated, he "trusted" me with the fact that he had no money, no job, a motorcycle, and a house that was going to be repossessed.

"I have dreams for us, but you deserve to be with someone *now* who can take you places you love, who has the clothes and a car to show you off," he would say. He wouldn't dwell on it, just drop it in the conversation when we were off to the Grandview movie theater after splitting the cost of happy hour snackies at the Green Mill, our favorite restaurant near the Saturday afternoon AA meeting where we met. Jack never had to bring it up again, because I was on it, solving the problem; in this case, wondering how I could tactfully and kindly offer him a double closet's worth of beautiful men's clothing that my first husband had left behind. I was even prepared to have it tailored for him! When I couldn't endure the angst any longer, I shared my thoughts.

"I don't think I could do that," Jack humbly responded. "That is really generous, but I wouldn't have any way to pay you for them. Thank you, though."

"Well, maybe just try on something and see if it even fits," I countered gently, totally unaware I was being played. "They are just hanging there. I don't need money for them, and I will be giving them away to someone. Think of it as a 'meant to be' solution that could be good for you and good for me. Well, just think about it."

And think he did for just the right amount of time, before stepping into a half a dozen suits; dress shirts, ties, belts, and shoes to match, straight off the cover of GQ.

The car situation was similarly solved by looking for a used Subaru Tracker for Jack that could carry karate gear from school to school where he taught his classes. That was our plan as we walked into the dealership in West St. Paul and somehow, in less than two hours, walked out with a white Miata for me and a plan to give Jack my fire-engine red Jeep Wagoneer - the one with the Classic gold spoke wheels and leather interior…more than suitable for Jack's traveling karate business.

At the end of two weeks, I had read 18 journals. I closed the last notebook and wept. I didn't want the books to end. Now there was just me. I was sorry it was over because in a much bigger sense so much was truly over. Whatever I thought I had was just…just…well, exactly what was that life I called my own? An illusion? Pretend? Make-believe? I recognized details, addresses, the names of my children, but I didn't know how to reconcile the story I read, where I had been or how I had gotten there. I thought I knew what was real, but now I doubted it all.

I sat. I breathed the night air slowly, in and out and in and out. I turned out the light and pulled the blankets around me so that I was warm. I knew

Numb and Alone which drifted in and out of Sad and Scared. And then as muddled as I was, a different feeling started to rise up in me, building slowly, gathering steam. I only had an inkling of what it was when my eyes, weary from reading, finally closed; not that being asleep mattered because the feeling kept coming. It was Fight.

When morning arrived, I awoke with a sense of clarity, especially when I saw William and Molly in the light of a new day. Their faces were the same faces I knew and had always known, faces that didn't change whether I read 18 journals or not; faces that I loved to make smile and for whom I had piles of adventures and plans; faces I delighted in teaching and introducing to a world that was wonderful. I loved those faces, and I had plans! Nothing was going to get in the way of great plans for their lives. Nothing. I was ready for the fight. You mess with my children, and you've got a fight.

Chapter 3
The Birthday Party

Life so far had been a whirlwind - a U-Haul move to the north woods, a phone call that decreased our family by 25%, and a box of journals filled with content I could never put back. So much for our family's plan to move to our cabin, the most wonderful place on the face of the planet. I got used to feeling numb much the time, when I was reading at night and when I was remembering what I had read the next morning. I didn't mind Numb. Numb was good. It took the edge off.

By week three, I had lost the short-lived rhythm of our new little life, Box Mountain by day and a darker climb by night. Life was unravelling and picking up speed. I was grasping for a plan, any plan, and had made a little headway on locating the AA meeting in Two Harbors as well as contacting therapists for each of us. That week, on June 6th, we celebrated Molly's 4th birthday, an event that introduced me to an important phenomenon: I could hold several realities at one time.

JOY at seeing my sweet, sweet daughter flit around Sammy's Pizza Parlor, delighted with extra cheese pizzas, marble cupcakes piled high with pink frosting and gifts from complete strangers: my sister-in-law's sister's children because they were the only family I could think of in Duluth that had young children and who sort of knew us, and who might be willing to come for an impromptu birthday celebration.

DEVASTATION and CONFUSION at seeing Jack unexpectedly arrive at the party, looking like Neil Diamond in a super-low, unbuttoned, V-necked, poly-something shirt, sporting an array of new gold chains hanging around his neck. If that wasn't enough, he complemented his look with some earth-mama, funky brown beads on his wrist where his watch used to be, beads that were somehow to be compatible with the overwhelming scent of what the heck was that??? Months later when visitation rules set in, I discovered it was Jack's mistress's perfume called "Angel." Sample size bottles arrived home in Molly's suitcase each time she visited her dad.

Anyway, "Angel" hung all over and around what was once my familiar husband, now turned good-time guy with a Pinky Lee personality. Choosing to skip the pleasantries of "Hello," when he made his grand entrance, Jack went right for Molly, scooping her up to swing her around, and then throwing her in the air. When she came down, he bounced her on the floor, jostling, tickling, all the time kidding with her "friends" who mostly asked, "Who are you?!"

FURY with Jack, who at my request, stepped outside to the parking lot, away from the party to answer a few questions.

"What exactly did you mean when you said you weren't coming up here at all? What does that mean for us?" I began not because I was curious or interested in his inner thoughts. I was hot and I wanted answers.

"I'm not sure." Jack replied, which made me even hotter.

"You don't want a divorce do you?" I hated that I was helping him out with what he didn't have the guts to say to me.

"Uh, yes." He mumbled.

"Are you kidding me? We just got married! I mean, what are you saying? Don't you love me anymore?!" I shouted. What was I saying? I'd read the journals. Of course he didn't love me. But, I was so confused and angry, clinging to denial, that all I could do was throw a tantrum. I couldn't adapt that fast. My body, my eyes and ears were still in the old plan, that he loved me.

"Well…" And after a long pause, "I'll always like you…I mean, you are the mother of my children." Jack said.

"Oh, my God! What?! Like me?! Are you crazy? Are you in love with someone else?"

"Probably."

"Probably?! Are you having an affair with Vanessa?"

"I don't think that's any of your business." Jack said calmly as if I could be dismissed.

"None of my business! I'm your wife!!"

I remember the rest as a lot of spluttering and fits and starts of sentences with one final in-tact thought I did manage to spit out. This one I delivered without any hesitation.

"I hate you for what you are doing to William and Molly."

DETERMINATION that we weren't going down. I returned to the party, shaking from what had just happened and from the gathering storm raging inside me. The disapproving looks on the faces of our guests took me aback at first. It took a moment, but I did finally realize that the parking lot was in full view from the pizza parlor front window. I guess the visual didn't measure up to great hostess behavior.

I wanted to care but I didn't. Instead, I slapped on a smile, apologized for having to step away for a few minutes, and sincerely thanked everyone for coming. I meant it. Molly had delighted in her birthday party; she had seen her dad and being four was off to a great start. At the last good-bye, the storm hit, and the dam broke. My spirit grabbed a sword, and I drew a line in the sand. *You fucker, you low life, you absolute loser, you fucking asshole! We are NOT going down. Get the hell out of my way. No matter what you do to me, you are not taking me down. And as for William and Molly, they will have great childhoods and great lives! So, get this, WE ARE NOT GOING DOWN!*

And then rivers of tears. Driving an hour home to the cabin trying not to make crying noises was the saddest and wettest I think I have ever been. I was glad it was dark, glad Molly was occupied with a toy and glad William was content listening to the radio.

NUMB settled in, that familiar, surrealistic wrapping around my life that kept me asking if this was really happening.

Looking back at this particular 24 hours, holding several realities at one time was a fascinating and important discovery for me. I relished this awareness. It was the first bit of good news I found myself mulling. Each feeling, each reality had been so intense that I could see them all clearly and distinctly. I found I didn't have to do anything; I could just tolerate them. Or I *could* do something, I could run with one of them.

I quickly found out what happened when I ran with rage, swinging at things I couldn't change or control until I reached the point of exhaustion. I also found out how happy I could be when I chose to play and create an adventure with William and Molly. It was all about holding different realities as if they were bundles of energy but choosing the one I wanted to live.

Choosing gratitude and joy when everything was definitely nuts, brought me peace.

Choosing to have a positive outlook on a situation gave me confidence that I would not drown in the overwhelmingly sad and devastating details of my life. The act of choosing, period, even when my choice didn't work out, brought me a sense of progress and that things were moving. Furthermore, if I made a mistake, I could make another choice, a better choice using what I learned from the first choice.

I began practicing making choices day-by-day and often, moment to moment, determined to steer our ship no matter what came our way. I felt in charge. I deliberately chose to make each day an adventure which, wait a minute, *committed me to being around the next day and the next day after that.* That realization was powerful. I never checked out and I had no plans to quit.

I never stopped owning my own life. I was learning to entertain separate realities, one of which tempted me to see myself as an absolute idiot who should just throw in the towel. But another of which invited me to chase our dreams - rich and wonderful and vibrant dreams for William and Molly and me. These were the places I wanted to go. Believing in our dreams brought laughter, joy and delight to the adventure of our new life. And so it was. Dreams. That's where I would take our new family in the midst of the rubble of a shattered family that was over.

Little did I know that I would look back on these beginning days as *mildly* confusing and relatively uncomplicated despite their excruciating pain. We needed some time so we could practice acknowledging loss and grief, bewilderment and disorder, unraveling and inertia while we chose adventure, joy, delight and gratitude

Chapter 4
Lists

Another day arrived and the details were the same. Just me. And William and Molly of course, who were still asleep. I didn't feel desperately alone in the quiet of the morning. The birds were awake, making their happy little chirping sounds and I was entertaining my first thoughts when a treasured voice from my memory joined me.

"You know, Annie, we humans are designed to live in 24-hour chunks of time," I recalled hearing as I sat at my Wednesday night AA meeting. It was the voice of a fellow alcoholic who was a little further down the road of recovery in the number of years he had been sober. He was my friend and I admired how he lived. I looked up to him, I listened to him, and I was always eager to learn from him.

He continued, "You can try and pack in more than a day can hold, but for me - when I take on too much, stop nourishing myself, stay up too late, worry, things don't go so well. When I take my life a day at a time and add in self-care, I tend to get better results."

"Yup," I nodded, "Thanks for the reminder."

I had been sober 19 years when we moved to the cabin, having never missed one of those Wednesday night meetings from the day I walked in. That was my home group, the place I returned again and again to learn how to live without drugs and alcohol, how to be honest, how to clean up my past and how to go forward as a better person. Gradually, I added two other meetings a week including Alanon, at the not so gentle suggestion of a dozen fellow alcoholics who were there Wednesday nights. But in those first months, I was terrified to miss AA because I had nothing else to keep me sober. As time progressed, I never missed because I desperately wanted to be accepted by a group of people I was coming to love, not understanding that I already was accepted and that my self-esteem just needed to catch up. Finally, I never missed because I came to understand that my time there was the best investment I could make in never drinking again, in continuing to grow spiritually and live responsibly, in giving to others and in having a decent chance at a life that was promised in sobriety - a life that was happy, joyous, and free.

I cannot remember that other committed members of my group missed Wednesday nights either, except for travel or being ill. We were a family. In return for perfect attendance, I was given hope, belief in the God of my understanding, consistency in my behavior, strength and a lifeline that was there for me, coursing through my blood and integrated in all I had become whether I was at the meetings or not. Gratefully, I didn't have to work very hard to access AA's perspective at the dawn of a new day in the same way I didn't have to work very hard to access organizational habits I had gained from twenty years of corporate work. So, paradoxically, I sat peacefully in my abysmal reality, making a list for the day because that's how I had lived for a very long time - secure in my faith that God had my back and confident in the power of a To Do list.

1. Talk to the North Star Association foreman, Mark, about the roof.

He was calm, Minnesota nice and straight to the point.

"The shingles in the 'V' are showing some wear which can probably be handled by patching - say, a hundred dollars' worth of materials and labor. You'll need an estimate. There are contractors who have done good work in the Association. Ask around."

"Okay! Thanks. I can take it from here," I answered as I proceeded to follow his directions exactly, not taking into account my naiveté, my blind spots regarding reference checks, or a second and even third opinion.

$17,000 later I had a completely new roof. Not because I needed one but because it never occurred to me that there were "a multitude of options you could have explored that would have saved you a ton of money! Why that's highway robbery!" commented *everyone* who stopped by to check out the new roof. *I thought I was extremely fortunate to be able to cover the roof with my savings and just between me and me, good job to me for handling it on my own.* I had $2,000 left over and furthermore, the new roof proposition sounded totally reasonable.

"It looks like the ridge cap ripped off in the storm of 1995. Water seeped in and all the timbers are rotten. You'll need to rebuild and re-roof ... *now*. You are in a dangerous situation," summarized the lucky contractor who already smelled opportunity when he pulled in my driveway. I had introduced myself with a short version of our catastrophe when I made the appointment for him to stop by and take a look. It didn't take him long to come to the rescue when I explained that I knew nothing about the roof or construction of the cabin. I listened and even felt lucky that the cabin wasn't collapsing.

"Okay, then. Well, let's get started," I said as I signed the contract, feeling accomplished in handling another tough situation. Note to self: Get additional quotes and reference check on future projects. Keep Mike in the loop.

2. Go to Two Harbors Courthouse and make sure cabin is in my name. It was.

3. Hire attorney, James Northland, hands down the best divorce lawyer in Duluth. My lawyer brother had advised me. "Get to Duluth, it's a bigger city. You'll need a big gun, and you should probably have someone from up there rather than a lawyer commuting from the Twin Cities."

"Agreed, I'll call right away," I said. It didn't matter. James' receptionist greeted me and then responded, "I'm sorry, he cannot speak with you as doing so would be a conflict of interest. He was retained by your husband, a Mr. Jack Stewart, earlier today."

"Shit," I mumbled to myself after thanking her. Note to self: Change "Hire James Northland" to "Find lawyer."

4. Call Chris and find out best grade schools for William and Molly. Chris had been recently hired as the new Assistant Head of School at St. Peter's School, the private, prestigious college-prep institution in Duluth. I knew Chris because his former position was Lower School Principal at St. Paul Academy where my older boys had attended. I was excited because we would be on the same page regarding a quality education.

5. Call Jack. Ask for money.

"When are you going to mail us a check? Do you remember that you are our sole source of support? By that I mean, you are the only one of the four of us in the family who has a job, so we are counting on you for the time being."

Who was I kidding? What a waste of time to even ask. Still, I did; denial was alive and well. I just couldn't imagine that because he said he was leaving, he would turn and walk and keep on walking.

There was never any money until our divorce was finalized eight months later and child support was established. We did entertain an unexpected visit three months later, this time at the Pizza Place in Two Harbors where we chose to celebrate William's birthday. After the other nine-year-olds and their families had said good-bye, Jack pulled up in a shiny, new, forest green Ford 150 pickup truck. We almost didn't recognize him until "Angel" wafted in, and the new set of bolder, gold chain neckwear gave him away. Smooth as ever, he paid for some video games with large bills in his new wallet and then drove off into the night leaving William and Molly broken-hearted after an hour's visit with the dad they still loved.

6. Go swimming.

7. Make an appointment with Human Services for family therapy.

8. Call Dain Bosworth in Two Harbors about my old Honeywell stock - anything left to cash in?
9. Find a church.
10. Join T-ball, soccer and swimming lessons.
11. Is bankruptcy a good idea?
12. Find Joy, the person.

And find Joy, I did. It only took one phone call to the last number I had for her. Joy, a lifelong friend from twenty years ago, now remarried and living an hour away in Aurora, Minnesota, arrived on our doorstep that coming weekend with a pickup truck full of groceries and a quarter cord of wood.

After hugs of excitement at seeing each other again, she moved quickly back toward the truck and said over her shoulder, "I had to shop, so I just figured that I would buy two of everything. This is Benny, my husband, and he got the wood." Never having been one to wait for unnecessary direction, Joy continued talking as Benny and I exchanged greetings, "Where do you want everything? Oh, never mind, I can just start putting things away in the obvious places."

As the first angel to swoop in, Joy set a high bar for those that followed. I had never been so needy and so I was unprepared for the generosity and goodness that came to Molly, William, and me. Seeing how deeply the children hurt without their dad all of a sudden was the worst for me. The abundance of kindness diluted that and sustained me while the healing began.

All summer long I made those lists, checking things off and dealing with the good, bad and the ugly that followed. Every day I made enough headway to keep going and every day was without question, an adventure.

13. Take the lawnmower to town for repair.

Chapter 5
Hello Two Harbors

We looked like a movie to me a lot of the time. Somewhere in my head I could hear the audience gasping, "Oh my God!" or dropping their heads, covering their foreheads and eyes with one hand, whispering "How pathetic, really" or nodding, eyes locked on us as we made our way into the world each day, emotionally affirming us and encouraging us by continuing to watch.

We had a "Leave it to Beaver" aura about us in our first few days as new residents of Two Harbors. I had problems that I needed to handle and so we would go to town. For example, we had a piece of junk for a lawn mower...another excessively expensive purchase for which I had plunked down my credit card. Jack found it at the Northern Store which was his Nordstrom's Shoe department. I knew I was in for it when the words "date night" appeared anywhere in his proposals.

"Hey, I have a place I really want to take you. Let's go out, have some dinner at Bakers Square and then I want to take you somewhere with me and show you something. No, no, no… I can't tell you more...it's a surprise…better than a movie…just the two of us…date night."

So, instead of a moderately priced lawn mower that cut grass, I now owned a $1,000 machine with an attitude. It had blades that defied sharpening. It required a complicated dance to start it and then only cut grass if you pulled it backwards. It had a pedigree: Honda. It accepted only high-end oil and gas, it had a grass-catching bag and height adjuster, it was a mulcher, it was capable enough to be another member of the family, and it was a pain in the ass.

In this new world of what should I do first, or next, or at all, getting the mower fixed seemed right. After all, I had a lawn that needed mowing. It was our home and I wanted to maintain it. It was up to me, and I was willing to do the work. I just needed a little help on occasion. In keeping with what June Cleaver would have done, I dressed the children in their summer shorts, insisted on washed faces and brushed teeth, put on a summer frock myself and a little blush and loaded that mower into the car to get help.

About the summer frock. Uh, not really. I owned no such thing, so I opted for khaki shorts and a white tee shirt, an okay outer layer hiding a frayed bra and men's underpants - not boxers - the real deal, thick cotton with the panel in front. It was the only box of such things I had unpacked, and I didn't want to spend any money I didn't have to spend; plus they were surprisingly comfy. Anyway, I bounced us into town in our white Ford Explorer, a vehicle with shock and suspension issues that would surely see the junkyard before I could pay it off. There was plenty of parking on the main street of Two Harbors, so we picked a spot across from the Dairy Queen and began walking up one side and down the other to get help for the lawn mower and to introduce ourselves.

Two Harbors, now a tourist town, had its history in the ore mining industry of the early 20th century. The town grew out of the natural harbor which allowed the huge ocean freighters to come ashore and receive their cargo while those that worked the boats found solace in one of the houses of ill repute. Two Harbors had its own tugboat, lighthouse, railroad station and community of farmers, fishermen and craftsmen who built its businesses, schools, and churches, primarily Lutheran. In addition to the Sioux, Cherokee and Iroquois, predominantly Scandinavian immigrants chose this special part of America to make their new home. Over time, the town grew up the shore and into the hills so that main street became the narrowed down version of Highway 61 when it passed through Two Harbors. For one mile there were two lanes with sidewalks on either side, like any other street in a small town. What wasn't like any other one-mile street in a small town was that the city planners approved four stoplights. It drove the tourists crazy.

For three quarters of a century, Two Harbors remained true to its historical roots which were colorfully represented by the store fronts in the mile of its main street - Highway 61. One stuffed grocery store finally gave way to Super One, but for all of my growing up years, it was locally owned and the place you learned to "drive" albeit an old, normal-sized shopping cart, around and through aisles crowded with boxes and customers. Religious bookstores outnumbered every other shop three to one, but there was plenty of room for local offerings: jars of honey, jam and homemade maple sugar candies, decor and furniture made of birch bark and carved wood, chainsaw carvings of over-sized eagles and bears - made to order right before your very eyes, Chinese take-out, one liquor and two clothing shops with home-made knitting, and beautifully tailored garments for every occasion, agate and stone jewelry, a couple of bars, and four cafes offering scrumptious homemade food and baked goods. It had its own unique charm, not a Cape Cod wannabe, rather a place on this earth that honored and valued the ingenuity, creativity and industry of its ancestors.

Big city folks that we were, but lovers of northern Minnesota, the children and I were ready to meet Two Harbors. Now this is where I should have heard those voices from the past coaching me about boundaries, appropriate things to share, who needs to know what…but reception in my brain wasn't too hot. My heart was so broken and bruised and hugely needy that I was only capable of moving from salve to bandage to kindness in any form it came our way. Nothing resembling discretion surfaced once we arrived at each destination - just my babbling from person to person.

Every conversation, and I do mean every, ended in the story of what just happened to us.

Short version: If I just needed to get to the point: "I just moved to Two Harbors with my two children. I drove up with the children. William? Molly? Say hello please, and my husband didn't show up. He drove another direction with a different woman and so I could use some help with this lawn mower."

Long to Longer Version: If it was early in the day and I was full of energy and talking with a kind and interested soul.

"I just moved to Two Harbors with my two children. William? Molly? Say hello please. We live in a cabin at North Star Association," (pausing ever so slightly to let the impression sink in or alternately, dropping the name and moving along in La-di-da fashion, "that we have used as a summer home for the last 10 years."

No need to explain to the locals that a "cabin" at North Star Association was not a deer shack in the woods sans indoor plumbing. It was one of 50 exclusive full-on rustic homes, half a million and up, in a gated community on the shores of Lake Superior. In some cases, the cabins like ours, were high up in the hills overlooking Her Majesty, while a few perched above the North Star River that ran north to south from the Superior Hiking Trail to the Lake. For all North Star Association members but us, it was one of many homes, usually a summer retreat, but not always. Some came to cross country ski in the winter, if their cabin was one of the few that was winterized.

Pausing ever so slightly to acknowledge the other person's "Hmm's," and take a breath, I continued,

"I actually grew up on the North Shore because my parents brought us up each year to stay for the month of August at Sve's Split Rock Cabins because we had hay fever so badly. We could breathe so much better with the air off the lake rather than from the land. We would stay until the night before school started. We shopped at the old Ben Franklin in town for school supplies and then we would head down to school in the Twin Cities hoping for an early frost. So, in a lot of ways it feels like coming home."

Full stop. Now waiting for their question or remark which inevitably had some key word that took me to what happened to us.

For example, they would say, "What made you decide to live here and leave the Cities?" And I would reply, "Well, my husband and I decided to be true to what was really important to us…a simpler life, time as a family, being on Lake Superior for more than just weekends and vacations and so we decided to downsize and move to the cabin. The only problem was that he didn't show up. So now I am here with the children and we still like the plan."

"What? How awful!!" And then we were off.

Long, longer, or short version, it didn't matter. Bottom line was I told everyone I met the basics and as much as they could take.
So, for at least two weeks, we alternated time at home unpacking the box mountain with meeting the merchants of Two Harbors. I usually had a lawn mower type issue of one sort or another to get us started and then off we would go to the post office, the gift shops, the hardware store, the grocery store, the DQ, the gas stations, the movie rental store, the shoe store, the library, the bakery, the antique shop, the bowling alley. We said hello to anyone we were standing next to in a line. If we made eye contact, I was introducing us.

To me it seemed like the right thing to do. I had been raised by Robert McMillan, Jr. whose signature social skill was "the handshake."

"Put your hand out. Say, 'Hi, I'm Annie McMillan.' Look them in the eye. Squeeze. Tighter. Say their name. 'It is very nice to meet you, Mr. Robertson.'"

I can't remember when I didn't know how to introduce myself. It was something I did on auto pilot all day long and so that's what I did in Two Harbors adding, "And these are my two children, William and Molly," at which point, to the best of their abilities, they shot their little hands out and said,

"Hi. Nice to meet you Missus msushsus."

Driving home with the mower planted in a shop for repair, or with new library cards or a list of the churches in town plus a day full of interactions, I felt successful. William and Molly had looked pained along the way, and I didn't like that.

"Do we have to stop and talk to everybody? Can't we just go back to the cabin now?"

"In a little while," I countered cheerily. "This is how we are going to make friends! Let's go see this place and find out who is in that shop. We'll swim soon...I promise. Come on, this will be fun!"

In hindsight, I know they had a point, a good point, and had they been able to articulate it, "Good God, Mom. Enough with the dad left us already!" maybe I would have heard them. But they were small, and I was trying to use the things I knew to help us begin again.

Here's what I knew. It beat doing nothing. It beat looking at the boxes all the time and unpacking in a cabin that was supposed to have a dad and husband there, too. It beat back the "You're fucked" assessment that was calling my name. And the truth is it *was* fulfilling for me to undoubtedly be too ridiculously open about all the details of this miserable little happenstance, because enough of the time, people really did listen and spent a moment with us before passing us along with compassion and encouragement and love.

I know they were just introductions and that we needed intimacy and depth and big fat tent ropes of emotional support, but we couldn't produce that like we could produce twenty or thirty new friends in a week of walking around. They weren't best friends...yet. They were our best friends so far.

It didn't really matter what anyone said to an introduction. If we hadn't met before there was always a segue waiting for me to give them enough to talk about at *their* dinner table. And that's what I think must have happened since shortly thereafter, I noticed that when I had a car accident (one of many) the guys at the gas station knew about it before I got to town to find a mechanic. That was true of any news about us. I didn't dare worry about whether we were a topic for gossip. I couldn't be bothered. I just hoped we were a topic of interest and candidates for support.

Chapter 6
My New Home Meeting

Twenty years into sobriety and on the heels of our little tour of introductions through the streets of Two Harbors, I found the local AA meeting. On Monday and Friday nights I gathered up William and Molly and was there when the meeting doors opened in the basement of our local hospital, Lakeland Memorial. It was an unexciting venue, a lot of light blue and beige hospital colors, and a meeting room at the bottom of the steps by the emergency room entrance. As AA meeting rooms go, it was predictable, decked out with some matching chairs, some not, and definitely not matching meeting tables, end tables and lamps. There was coffee. There was a door on the room. Perfect.

It didn't particularly bother me that I didn't know anyone. I was used to that about AA and I was getting very used to that in Two Harbors. I did notice that I was the only female in a group of fifteen men. Big Deal. Oh, and that the average age looked to be about 85. Another Big Deal. I was sure that I was going to be at home here and that I could openly share the mess I was in. So sure, that I told my group about the journals I had found.

Before I read a little excerpt, it occurred to me as I looked around the room of men that maybe I might be totally naïve about a whole lot of things and that here I had a group of men who would be honest with me. After I opened with who I was and who we were, myself and the children, I continued,

"I know I can be naïve and maybe I am making a big deal about these journals when this is the way guys are. They just don't tell women, or *this* woman, meaning me, about their fantasies, and that Jack's writing here is normal; normal, healthy sexuality, you know, normal."

As I opened the spiral bound notebook and read, my group seemed suddenly formal, sitting on all sides of the rectangular table, most hands folded, resting on the table in front of chests in plaid lumberjack shirts, eyes looking down as they listened. They didn't bat an eye. They didn't shift in their seats as I read. True to the protocol of an AA meeting, they let me have my turn to talk. They made their point, however, when the person sitting next to me whose turn to speak was next, broke with tradition and turned his head enough to make eye contact with me. With one small side-to-side move of his head, he said quietly, "Not normal." As if well-rehearsed, the rest of the group breathed a sigh in unison, uttering soft grunting noises accompanied by the same head move, ever so slightly, side-to-side. I took that as unanimous, "not normal," and the meeting went on.

They say in AA that you should look for a home group by trying a few different meetings. Stay with one for six weeks or so to see if it fits you and if you like it. I didn't want to look any further. I liked it here. I liked what they grunted to me. These were my neighbors and I left that first meeting with the reminder from a particularly cantankerous looking fellow to take it a day at a time. I could do that.

"Keep coming back," I heard as I walked to the parking lot with William and Molly who had entertained themselves in the room outside the meeting with markers and paper and old Good Housekeeping magazines. Yup, we'd be back… for years to come.

Chapter 7
80% of Life is Showing Up

Delivering on my fist shaking promise, "William and Molly will have a great life!" required follow through. The strategy that came most naturally to me was to get out there and do stuff. Join something. Always have a plan for the day. Find out what our town of Two Harbors had to offer. Pick something and participate. I agreed with Woody Allen, "80% of life is showing up." I still agree.

As far as my selection criteria for filling the summer days, the bar was low because doing something, anything, was better than doing nothing. Furthermore, being busy was personal insurance against downtime when fear could slip in and take hold. I couldn't allow that because once that started, I knew I was a goner.

"I mean, come on!" I would hear someone at the board meeting in my head, screaming. *"You're so screwed. You've got nothing! This is over. You're over!!!"*

If it had been just me, I might have listened to those voices, but that was absolutely unacceptable when it came to the lives of William and Molly. They were going to have great lives, plus I did not want to be "over" so I was all about getting into action as early in the day as possible and running right up until bedtime.

I picked up a summer activities mailer from Lake County and started putting check marks by everything that we fit. In no time both children had joined the YMCA swim team. Molly became a member of the Sunshine Club, a song and dance troupe of girls 3 to 13, and the youngest addition to the preschool soccer club. With a few more phone calls, William joined the Cub Scouts and Summerblue Arts, a three-week day camp all about the arts. Altogether our summer calendar was filling out nicely and those great lives were starting to take shape.

We were also in the right place at the right time for "Heritage Days" about which I inquired when the children and I were picking out grass seed at the hardware store.

"Heritage Days? Why, it's the best summer festival in northern Minnesota, Wisconsin and even Michigan," Rob, owner of the store began with a big grin. Unable to contain his enthusiasm, he launched into a description, gaining in speed, volume and arm gestures until he had the full attention of everyone in the store. Feeling a little sorry I had asked, I wondered if he had watched Harold Hill in "The Music Man" one too many times.

"Two Harbors' Heritage Days! Friday through Sunday. We've got everything. A parade that *anyone* can join - just make a float! Marching bands that come from all over because they have such a good time here. Imagine! Two full blocks, right downtown here by the train depot, both sides of the street filled with booths of antiques, crafts, wood carvings, pottery, agate jewelry, homemade sweaters, pickled veggies and syrups from the sap of our very own trees; plus, local talent performances, pie eating contests and the best food round the clock that you can imagine. You'll have a great time. Mark your calendar - July 22nd!"

Rob took a breath and concluded not because he was finished, but because a new customer's, "Ahem!" clearly signaled he had been waiting a little too long. Curious about the pie eating contest as a possibility, I noted when and where we needed to be in order to win a brand new Schwinn bike.

During our first month in Two Harbors, we also sampled churches and joined the Two Harbors United Church, our best Presbyterian option. Finally, North Star Association had an 80-year-old tradition, The Lodge Talent Show, performed one night in August to a packed house of association families. Acts were heavy on singers who were related to each other, strumming ukeleles, guitars or the occasional banjo.

"And now what we've all been waiting for, 'The River Boys,' or 'Bards of the Woods,' or 'Sing for your Supper' or just, "Heeeeere's Rick!" We knew what was coming, we knew to sit back and get ready for our local Kingston Trio, North Star Association's Burl Ives or some variation on Peter, Paul and Mary." This summer, I signed us up despite the fact that I had no idea what we would call ourselves, let alone do. All I know is that every time we went to the lodge and saw "The Stewart Family" on the list of acts, we were validated as having a future.

All in all, I thought our summer selections had real possibilities for many days filled with fun. In fact, I could guarantee it because my philosophy of starting something new also included stopping when it wasn't fun anymore. I don't mean I encouraged "quitting" like school or homework or a sports team where there is legitimate commitment, but in most of these cases, we were in and stayed if it was fun or we were out. Summer turned out to be a series of experiments that despite their higher-than-expected failure rate kept us engaged and laughing.

YMCA Swimming

"We already know how to swim," William started as I drove my squeaky clean, wet-haired swimmers away from the Y to Dairy Queen for the promised treat. "And besides the coach isn't nice. I don't want to learn the butterfly and I hate the backstroke because I hit the wall when I'm doing the flip turn. My knuckles are bleeding. Look at them, Mom."

Molly followed, "The water is too cold, and I can't reach the bottom of the pool. The cap hurts my hair, and I don't want to swim that long. I can't reach the handles in the shower and the big girls won't help me make it warmer."

I was afraid this might be coming because I already had gathered my own data, sitting in the parents' viewing area above the pool, watching and offering many thumbs up with smiles of encouragement in an attempt to diffuse the snake eyes directed at me.

"How about this?" I began. "We can go to Open Swim at the pool in Two Harbors and I can help you with your flip turn, William. And Molly, I will go with you to the locker room and help you get your swim cap on so it doesn't pull your curls, plus I can meet you afterwards and we'll get the shower temperature right."

Quiet followed, except for William, "I'm hungry." "Me too," added Molly.

"Well, first things first. Let's add a couple of hotdogs and fries to our DQ order," I responded in an attempt to score a point. I sat us at the picnic table outside the Dairy Queen at the edge of Two Harbors and watched that familiar, "swimming makes me sooooo hungry" reaction to food. While my children happily gobbled, I thought in silence, *This is tough. William's and Molly's experiences are adding up to no fun ...so far. But Y's are filled with saints aren't they?*

When I was ten years old, I loved the Midway YMCA's 'Family Night.' That was the best Friday of the month because we bundled into our station wagon - Mom, Dad and four kids. When we hit the gym, we played whatever we wanted. I remember running to the big trampoline, playing basketball, badminton, and ping pong with Dad until we all met in the pool for swimming. The Y had a huge pool with room enough for all kinds of families, moms and dads and bunches of kids of all ages, and lots of chlorine. We were always the last to leave in sweet exhaustion.

Favoring my memory, I broke the silence.

"Doesn't food taste just so good after you have been swimming?" I asked, happy to see their nodding heads and smiles. "You know, both your teachers at the Y said you were really getting the hang of it and they would like to have you on the team if you wanted to try a swim meet. Shall we think about that and give it another try?

More quiet. Maybe William and Molly just wanted to eat or maybe mentioning a swim meet had some appeal or maybe they were just too tired to make their points again. All I know is that they hung in there, up to and through one swim meet.

William told me years later, that he was so nervous he ran to the bathroom a couple times to throw up before his race. Molly, who was supposed to be able to swim the length of the pool *and back,* dog paddled for two or three strokes and then rested by holding onto the side of the pool until she ventured out to take her next two or three strokes. That little rhythm stopped being cute when the pool was empty for several minutes except for Molly. Even the parents who cheer for everyone petered out until the last "Keep going! You can do it!" tailed off and we sat in stillness.

I looked around, fielding glares from William, and shrugs from both Molly's coach and the parent volunteer timer. Finally, Molly finished. Some dear soul in the bleachers stood up and gave her a standing ovation while an unbelievable number of the rest of the crowd followed. Molly beamed and I was grateful for the generosity of swim team parents.

That meet did turn out to be our grand finale, despite the fact that William won a trophy and Molly, a participant ribbon. Swimming after that was in our own Lake Superior at Serenity Point or in Eagles Nest Pool, the natural swimming hole in the North Star River just before her waters joined the big lake. Eagles Nest Pool became our favorite location for ending all fair-weather summer days. There was nothing better than skipping baths, heading for Eagles Nest, *making* ourselves get in the cold water, and then hurrying home to jump into our pajamas for a bedtime story and a cup of hot chocolate.

The Sunshine Club

Molly graced the stage as a Sunshine girl for two summers, during which she was a bright star despite the fact that the other Sunshine girls were significantly older. Molly reminded me of a little water bug on stage. She wore the same costumes, danced the same choreography, and had more enthusiasm than anyone else, *and* she was half as tall as the next shortest dancer. With her head up, shoulders back *and* a deep breath she approached but did not surpass any of the other girls' waists. Fortunately, Molly never had that view so as far as she was concerned she was a bonafide, full fledged, fully decorated member of the club. All was well from her perspective, looking into the audience of smiling attendees. Molly was in her element, belting out one tune after another. She made us proud and brought the house down at every performance.

The Sunshine Club performed up and down the north shore from Silver Bay to Duluth, which meant that senior centers, church groups, a few parents, neighbors, William and I were treated to thirty minutes of "action" songs at least once a week. "There's a Hole in your Bucket" "Do Your Ears Hang Low?" and "B-I-N-G-O" were some of the girls' best numbers because they included choreography for feet in addition to hand movements.

I came to dread mentioning to William that the Sunshine Club had a performance coming up.

"Nooooooo. Please Mom, I can't take it! Do I have to go?" William pleaded.

"Yes, and with a good attitude. We are going to be there for each other. You may bring a book. And yes, we can get a Dairy Queen."

I understood. I felt the same way except I had that mother gene of loving to see my children perform. I had to admit I was ready to bolt at the big finale: a sing-a-long featuring "You are My Sunshine" and "Keep on the Sunny Side." That did us in every time.

Pre-School Soccer

Molly played a whole summer season of soccer without ever touching the ball. She loved the outfit, the socks, the weensy little shin pads and her extra small soccer shoes. Even when her coach stopped the game and said to all the other kids,

"Let's let Molly have a turn to kick the ball," Molly shook her head and remained content to barely run, wandering up and down the sidelines picking clover.

From William's point of view this was a step up from the Sunshine Club because he could bring a book and lie in the grass plus it included Dairy Queen. I met a couple of nice parents, single stragglers who meandered up and down the sidelines with a dog or a newspaper. I also had my first introduction to the Two Harbors Moms Club, loosely but exclusively organized for Two Harbors born and bred moms. The experience was familiar, the same feelings I had my first day at a new junior high school in seventh grade. The moms in the club stayed to themselves, backs turned 3/4 away from me, talking softly with bursts of laughter as they alternated looking over their shoulders to see if I was still there, I guess. Their body language made their message clear,

"You weren't born here. You're not from Two Harbors. You don't belong in our inner circle, and you never will."

"Okay, got it" I remember thinking to myself. *"I mean really, who cares? We're not talking about Paris. This is Two Harbors for God's sake."*

Cub Scouts

William went once. I could see the "get me out of here" expression on his face the minute he turned toward the car when I arrived to pick him up. So much for hoping to see a happy boy with other happy boys enjoying a scout meeting in a Two Harbors backyard marked by big oak trees and a fire pit.

This was a John Candy movie gone wrong, complete with a portly scoutmaster in shorts, belt cinched to hold up the belly, unsuccessfully "leading" a frenzied pack of sweaty eight-year-old boys in uniforms whose shirts were hanging out, and cheeks were bright red from racing around the backyard. William was off to the side, away from the center of the pack, not that it was hard to find him since he was making a beeline toward me as soon as he saw my car round the corner.

"No, Mom, please no. No camping trip." I could hear as William approached the car. "We have to sleep in tents, and I don't know anybody. There are knives and ghost stories, plus we have to cook on a fire outside. You said we were just trying things. I tried. I don't like it. Everybody pushes everybody and the clothes are dumb," he continued non-stop as he crawled in the front seat.

As a seasoned camper myself, I could see his point. The Dennis the Menace visual simply didn't comport well with camping tools of the trade or safety. Even the smell of the backyard fire, evoking memories of starry nights, still waters, and glowing embers of a fire dying down on an island in the boundary waters, couldn't displace my own sense of danger looking at the scene before us. Maybe Boy Scouts could have been workable if the pack of boys had been friendly, but they were not.

"Hey, scouts!! Listen up!! I said listen up! LISTEN UP!" bellowed the scoutmaster. Nobody listened up but that didn't matter. What followed was a string of barked orders and shrill blasts which came from the shiny silver whistle that hung from a lanyard around the scoutmaster's neck, made presumably during craft time on the previous camping trip.

One and done. And of course, Dairy Queen.

Summerblue Arts

Judging by its credentials, Summerblue Arts looked to be a sure winner. The name alone suggested a level of sophistication beyond our other activities. In five years Summerblue Arts had earned a reputation for the mama of all day camps, a must do activity for forty kids providing their families could afford it. In our case, it was out of the question, costing more than any of our other choices by a factor of ten. That is, until Joan who was a new friend at church and mother of the program's director, gave William a scholarship. William was "in" which was a welcome change of pace. Summerblue Arts owned the cool factor in Two Harbors and automatically bestowed inclusion upon all its participants.

Summerblue Arts' 30-year-old director, Luke, was Joan's son who had been at the helm for five years. Luke returned each year with a staff of theater, art, dance, and music majors from colleges outside of Minnesota. Attracted to a counselor experience on the shores of Lake Superior, these kids were fun and friendly, relaaaaaaxed in their cut-off designer jeans, madras and tie-dyed accessories. They had interesting names like Sasha and Jules, complete with funky glasses, free hair styles, and a vibe that included a lot of slow head nodding. Their message from day one was gentle and inviting - Summerblue Arts is open for self-expression, the farther out, the better. Everyone is welcome.

Because it was a program for 7–17-year-olds, Molly and I were on our own to swim, hunt for agates or hike until it was time to pick up William either at the high school, which was condemned to demolition in the fall, or the circus-size white tent pitched in the fields three miles out of town across from Birch Bay.

William made new friends and was fun to watch in the presentation of their final artistic project. Families and friends were invited to a play the kids had written and produced. It was plotless, as I recall. Nevertheless, William went happily every day, packing his lunch, swimsuit and towel. Summerblue Arts was our no-drama, pun intended, July filler. Nothing wrong with that. We needed laid back and some nice, friendly college kids.

Heritage Days and the Pie Eating Contest

For a small town, Two Harbors had an impressive number of outdoor venues to show off its talent. Thomas Owens Park in the middle of town proudly surrounded the oldest bandshell in America where the oldest city band in Minnesota played Thursday night concerts all summer. Forty early comers occupied two rows of wooden benches that sat in front of the bandshell stage while at least one hundred families spread out on blankets across the groomed lawn behind and to the sides of them. The park covered one half of a city block which provided plenty of room for little kids to run and dance; late comers to make a comfortable entrance, and kids of all ages to line up for ice cream cones or Dilly Bars offered free of charge to everyone before the concert master took the stage at 7:30.

For smaller performances there was the more intimate stage near the harbor, overlooking the pier, the lighthouse and Her Majesty, Lake Superior. During Heritage Days, this was the main stage. Fiddling groups, Stacy's Dance School, the Sunshine Club and the Pie Eating Contest were assigned to times in the afternoon, reserving the evening for dancing under the stars.

On Saturday afternoon of Heritage Days William, Molly and I made our way to the stage near the harbor and joined the crowd already seated on the benches in front of the stage. It was nearing 3:00 and the crowd was sparse…maybe 50 moms and children, a few dads and grandparents. By contrast the street by the train depot was bustling with families crowded around the craft booths, hands already carrying the best kettle corn on the north shore, snow cones, hotdogs and giant chocolate chip cookies.

It was a July day made to order, sunny and 80 degrees with a slight breeze off the lake. After welcoming everyone to Heritage Days and the Pie Eating Contest, in particular, Mr. Emcee reached out toward the audience with open arms and a big smile,

"Alright everyone, who wants to come on up here to see who can be the fastest pie eater at Heritage Days? It has been a while since lunch, so it's a good time for a snack, don't you think? And today, if you are the winner of the kids' contest, you will win a new bike donated by TruValue Hardware! And if you are our adult winner, you will win a $100 gift certificate also donated by our friends at TruValue Hardware!"

While moms were encouraging their kids and the buzz of the crowd took over, Mr. Emcee wheeled the bike to the front of the stage and continued,

"Everyone who is 5-8 years old, boys and girls, brothers and sisters, cousins - everyone is welcome! Come on up here and we'll see who is going to ride this beauty of a bike home!"

In short order, Mr. Emcee had five volunteers up on stage, standing behind a red checkered tablecloth covering a long table borrowed from the nearest church basement. Each child had an empty medium pie tin in front of them. Given their heights they didn't have to lean down or over very far - a good thing - since the rules were designed to give the advantage to little ones.

"Okay everyone, you look great! Here are the rules. Put your hands behind your back while I fill the pie tins with whipped cream," he began as he proceeded down the row filling each pie tin with a moderate amount of circles of whipped cream.

"When I say, 'Go!' Lean forward and eat all of your whipped cream pie. The first one to finish is the winner. Any questions? I guess not. Good! Okay moms and dads, grandmas and grandpas let's hear you cheer. Kids, clasp your hands behind your backs. On your mark, get set GO!"

It didn't take long until a 7-year-old red head yelled "I'm done! I'm done!" to which Mr. Emcee said, "Yes, you are!" as he held up a licked clean pie tin and added, "We have a winner."

While the prize details and the winners circle festivities took over, William and I looked at each other with an identical reaction. We didn't need to speak, but did anyway,

"We've got this!"

"Yeah. Cake. Shall we both volunteer?"

"Why not?"

Meantime, Mr. Emcee's assistant was clearing off the pie tins, whipped cream cans and wiping off the tablecloth before setting up for round two.

"Congratulations again to our winner, Freddie Glasso. And now onto our adults! I need 5 volunteers to bring their appetites to the stage and show us how it's done. A $100 shopping spree at Ace Hardware awaits you."

William and I shot our hands up in the air as Mr. Emcee acknowledged us and told us to come on up.

"Stay here and cheer like crazy, "I told Molly and followed Mr. Emcee's hand directions to my spot, the end of the table. William was in spot one, then three high school boys, then me. My view from the stage was a sea of faces, many of whom seemed to be looking at me while talking softly to their neighbors. It occurred to me that perhaps, just perhaps, I was in a picture in which I didn't belong. But, at that point, I didn't have the luxury of caring, so I stood a little taller and assumed a ready posture. Assuming we already knew the rules I was confident until Mr. Emcee began, "We want to say a special thank you to the Vanilla Bean for providing their famous French Crumb Apple Pies for the adult contest. For anyone, and I'm pretty sure that's everyone in Two Harbors, who has had this famous pie, you know this is going to be one tasty contest." And then turning toward the five of us, he set a whole 10" French Crumb Apple Pie before each of our places a little more toward the center of the table so we had a ways to go to even get to the pie. I actually   appreciated that, once I was in the thick of it, literally, as that angle was gentler on the back. There was no time to even make eye contact with William although I tried. I just thought to myself, "Good God. Oh well, we're up here now." And then, "Hands behind your back. On your marks, get set, "GO!"

I dove into my pie, full face plant, mouth wide open.

"You're not working with me," I thought when my pie yielded not one iota. Cinnamon, sugar and butter crumb topping plugged my nostrils. Having taken what I thought was a huge bite, I came up for air. The pie looked the same. I hadn't made a dent. There is not much more to report for my efforts. I couldn't really gulp it down because it was so dense. Apples, even well-cooked apples, require some chewing. I looked down the row, trying to see how William was doing, but the bobbing bodies didn't yield a decent view. So, I just kept diving, chewing and swallowing at a pace that hardly felt like a race. The guy on my right actually won. I had my hands, make that mouth, full with my own pie, so I didn't notice anything other than he was defensive linebacker material in an "at the trough" posture for the whole event. I was actually happy to lose and relieved when he choked out, "I'm done."

Mr. Emcee gave us wet towels and thanked us for being good sports. I was happy to make a quick exit behind William who was quicker. I started, "Honey, how was I to know they were going to be real pies? I only made a little crater in the top of my pie. I'm sorry! By the way how did you do?"

"Not well. I don't even like apple pie. I never reached the bottom. It's okay, Mom, let's just go."

Molly wasn't old enough to be embarrassed by our performances. I couldn't stop laughing as William and I described our separate but all too similar realities all the way home. The only one having dinner was Molly while long into the evening, William and I continued to repeat the same question,

"How did that guy do it?!!!!"

The Lodge Talent Show

We were a talented family with years of "stage time" in the form of charades, school and church plays, dance, and singing in the car. We were seasoned, performance ready as far as I was concerned, only challenged by the up-and-coming Talent Show because we would have to pick just one act per person from our many possibilities.

We went with sure winners. Molly resurrected a tap dance performance to "Singing in the Bathtub," in which she broke out with an Al Jolson type ending, dropping to one knee, arms outstretched while she lip-synced to Mandy Patinkin's recording. She was good as gold.

William had earned his black stripe belt in karate and could impress the heck out of an audience especially in his crisp white uniform where the setting was up close and personal. William had mastered and performed a routine that included num-chuks, highflying kicks, spins in midair and loud karate yells. William was more than ready to go. Two acts down.

As for me, I pulled out a number from a past fundraiser I had chaired. Dressed in a black leotard, black tights, and a white line cook's apron, I gyrated to "Hot Stuff" a la "The Full Monty" waving kitchen utensils like I was in my own kitchen having a moment.

On the night of the talent show, I followed the children who flawlessly launched our family's North Star Association performance career. In my case, I think it was the quick turn toward the audience, the shimmy and the pelvic thrust that produced the audible gasp from the Association's finest. There was laughter too, so I kept going to the bitter end.

I decided to take the Emcee's comment as a compliment,

"Well, thank you to the Stewart Family! I think it is safe to say that in the many years of talent shows here in the Lodge, the moose on the wall has never seen anything quite like this."

William's and Molly's acts were met with hurrays and loud clapping. The applause after my act had an unmistakable ring to it like everyone was glad it was over. I didn't care. I enjoyed myself up there and the kids were great. Furthermore, the next day I got a thank-you note from Tootsie B., the matriarch of one of the founding families, a highly respected member of the inner circle of North Star Association, and accomplished artist. Tootsie wrote,

"I am still laughing! That was the best performance of any kind in all of the talent shows I've been to in over 50 years. Thank you, Annie."

Looking back at those first three months, no one could say we didn't give it a good try. No one could say we weren't good sports with adventurous spirits. No one could say we didn't make the best out of surprising situations. Not one of us ever ended the day with "I give up." Nope. That didn't happen. We were still standing.

In the midst of the cool air Her Majesty ushered in each evening to encourage us to end the day, She gently settled the sadness into our lives that was also ours. There were tears because we missed our old family, our dad, our life that seemed altogether. That was okay. Tears came at different times for each of us but mostly at night. The beauty was in moving from hours of experiences we had never had before, laughing and sometimes vowing *never* to do that again, into the stillness of the night, snuggling with each other and a bedtime book, while we learned to accept that all of it was ours. We loved each other. We were learning to be there for each other. We closed our eyes holding hands, I, in the middle, a child on each side letting the night do its healing.

Chapter 8
The Affair

"Good evenin', Max speakin'," I heard as the familiar and distinctly gentle voice answered the phone. Max was Vanessa's husband whom I called one night after supper two months into my new life.

"Hi Max. This is Annie McMillan Stewart."

"Hey, Annie. How are you?"

"Well, I'm okay. Listen, I just wanted to call. I hope it's okay. I've thought about you a lot - and the girls - what I mean is that when people have called me because they've heard that Jack left, and they want to support me, they also ask about you, I mean they don't know you but they'll ask, 'What about Vanessa's family? How is her husband doing? Two girls? Oh my God, what a shame.' I mean, you know. Anyway, I just wanted to say that I am really sorry," I rambled until I ran out of breath.

"Well, hey, it's not your fault," Max responded, true to the gentleman he was.

"I know," I continued, "but I'm just really sorry for your family, too. So, anyway, I hope it's okay that I called. Um…how are *you* doing?"

"Oh, probably about as good as you are," he answered with unmistakable sadness in his voice.

It was at that moment that the pain and loss were very real for me. Max was like a mirror, heartbroken, in a newly configured family of three, left behind with his children, picking up pieces, looking at a very different future than they thought they would have. Me too. Us too, free floating in that same place of grief. Looking at a future…what future? Our two remnants of families - still standing, barely, even though we had the wind knocked out of us. For my part, I knew what I had said to my two children, and my two children were counting on me to chart our course, to deliver on my promise, "We will be okay. We will be more than okay."

Max and I were different people having the same experience, a good enough reason to begin a friendship of wounded warriors who, as Max said, "might have been fooled once, but are not dumb." We connected by phone, speaking often, comparing notes, sending copies of affidavits, comparing where the money was and wasn't going, even connecting our two lawyers so they could compare the asset pictures Vanessa and Jack were submitting as evidence of Jack's position of hardship. Oh puhleeeeze. Vanessa was a multi-millionaire and Jack needed one. What hardship?

I also hungered for the sizzling details. I admit it. I wanted to know what happened and how I could have missed it all. The bottom line, "He had an affair," just didn't do it for me. As it turned out Max and I spent our conversations reconstructing the past year, walking back through different periods of time with what we both knew, putting together pieces of "The Affair" puzzle that had eluded us both. It wasn't that hard to figure things out. Max was a pretty cool cat about the whole thing while I know I contributed muffled gasps and audible, "Are you kidding me?" responses to what became obvious. It seemed that Jack and Vanessa did little to hide their affair, spending time together with extended families, each other's children, friends, neighbors, and at each other's work and play environments. I guess they thought no one would get it. They were right. I didn't notice, I didn't suspect, I never imagined that Jack would or could leave us - not me, not our marriage, not two beautiful, amazing children, not our story and not our dreams. Max, too; he was duped. We had both watched and I had enabled the oddest requests, always dismissing them as just that, odd.

I met Vanessa at The Decathlon Club when she and Jack "ran into each other" watching our two families' children swim in the pool. Conveniently, I was up on the track running two miles, appreciative that Jack was willing to keep an eye on the children. When I came down to the pool, I met Vanessa who was busting - pun intended - out of her two-piece swimming attire. That didn't prevent her, however, from enthusiastically jumping up to say, "Here's a spur of the moment thought! Why don't you, Annie, Molly, William, and Jack join Mr. Max (that is what she called her husband) and me, Jenna and Nancy for lunch? It's on me. We have been wanting to spend some time to get to know your family and we've all got to eat, right? Their burgers and chicken fingers are great. How about it - say noon?"

A pause ensued, long enough for Jack to look at me with his, "Why not?" expression and for me to look back with, "Okay, why not?"

After another briefer pause, I spoke for our family, "Spur of the moment it is! Thank you very much. We'd love to join you."

This dynamic, where ostensibly Jack deferred to me to make the decision he wanted, was a pattern I didn't identify until I learned about the roles of predator and prey and specifically the techniques of grooming. I just thought he was respectful of my wisdom regarding what was best for our family, or comfortable with me being the extrovert while he was the more strong, silent type. Jack was very skilled in getting me to behave in his favor without me feeling manipulated. That morning he made sure I got everything I wanted: some extra time to sleep in, a latte delivered to me when I got out of the shower, time to myself to work out and run, lots of compliments and flirting so that by the time something nice happened for him - running into a parent of a student in his karate class - I was only too happy to say, "Okay, why not?"

Vanessa's birthday party, the next event we were invited to attend, had its own peculiarities. After we said yes to the invitation, which was interestingly also at the Decathlon Club in one of their party rooms, Jack announced on the night that he was just too tired to go.

I didn't suspect anything and asked him out of concern, "Are you sure? Do you think you are getting sick? Is there anything I can do?"

"No not really," answered Jack. "It has been a long week; I just don't want to go out again. I'm out of gas, and I just need to stop. I'm sorry. I don't want to stop you from going, though."

"Okay, sure," I said. "I understand." And then thinking out loud I continued, "The children are excited, it is a party, and I think they will be disappointed if I tell them we're not going. Plus, I don't feel good about canceling at the last minute. I don't really want to go without you - it was the family outing I was excited about."

Jack didn't say anymore. He didn't have to. He knew me and that I would do the considerate thing. "Okay, I think we'll go. We'll go now - be the first ones there and then get home early, too."

Vanessa's face dropped when we arrived at the party room without Jack.

"Oh no, can you call him?" she begged. "Maybe he's feeling better by now.

He HAS to come - it's my birthday and he promised." So rather than a normal reaction on my part, "What are you, seven? You are an adult, and another adult has said he will not be able to attend your party tonight," I said instead, "Alright, let me give him a try and maybe he'll reconsider."

And sure enough, with a little coaxing, Jack made the effort to come to the party. I will never forget Vanessa's reaction when I told her Jack was on his way.

"He's coming?" she exploded as she threw her arms around me in an excited hug. "Oh Annie! I love you! Thank you so much for getting him here!"

The party was a nothing party –- a Decathlon prepared spread of meatballs, potato chips, carrot sticks and dip, a single layer cake with writing on it, and about 15 people to sing Happy Birthday. We still went home early. If more happened that night for Jack and Vanessa, I didn't know about it. I hadn't caught on. It was just an evening with new friends, and I wasn't looking for anything.

After those two experiences, lunch and a birthday party at the Decathlon Club, my expectations regarding "anything Vanessa" hovered around tasteless mediocrity. I didn't just arbitrarily relegate her to that category, she earned it. Her excessive bling, her slicked back, short blond hair, her orange-red, long gel nails had tempted me for a short time to conclude that here was a woman of glamor and possibly sophisticated taste. But she was a ditz. When the invitation came to attend Max's 50th birthday party, I wasn't excited. I had been to the party she planned for herself!

This time Vanessa was planning a big surprise for her husband at a special place - wait for it - The Decathlon Club - specifically, the party room with the parquet dance floor. Even though Max clearly told his family that he didn't want a party because he was going skydiving in Wisconsin with some army buddies and planned to get back pretty late, Vanessa planned a surprise party.

It was a surprise party, alright, especially for the guests who arrived at five and were still waiting for the guest of honor at ten. The Decathlon Club had done its best to feed everyone with another buffet, suitable for children so this time there were some additional goodies like chicken tenders and French fries…otherwise, same meatballs, same carrot sticks, same dip. The open bar helped, but really, all combinations of conversational pairs were on their third round. There just wasn't more to say, eat or drink, so people started putting on their coats and rounding up their children. Of course, that was the moment Max arrived and blended into his own party without missing a beat. Everyone save a few tea-totalers were at the same level of inebriation, so it didn't really matter what party you had been at, you were now at this party where the DJ started playing tunes and encouraging the crowd onto the dance floor.

"Happy Birthday Max! You are 50, man! That is so awesome. Let the night begin. Come on everybody. Bring it to the dance floor. Put that coat down - we need you up here, brother!" A few people responded, but not enough for the DJ who added, "Listen up, you party animals. Let's start out with a Ladies' Choice. Vanessa, would you do the honors?"

No one except possibly the birthday boy himself, was as surprised as I was to watch Vanessa breeze by me as she picked Jack while over her shoulder she tossed, "May I dance with your husband?"

"Sure!" I automatically responded because you are already! And then in a moment of brilliance added, "Here's the guy I want for my dancing partner!" pointing to eight-year-old, William, who broke into a grin while his three-year-old sister, Molly, cried, "Me, too. Me, me, me, too." We made it a threesome, a busy little dancing threesome that came together in the spur of the moment to have fun at the party. Little did I know that was to be our configuration in the near future: Jack andVanessa. William, Molly, and me.

The "Affair Before Our Very Eyes" had one last spectacular evening, The Italian Dinner Party *not* at The Decathlon Club. In mid-May Vannessa sent an invitation home with Jack for our families to have dinner at their house. Mr. Max was planning on cooking one of his famous Italian dinners, and Vanessa hoped we would come early so the kids could play together.

At five o'clock the next Friday night we arrived at the modest home of Vanessa and Max a block or two from Lake Nokomis. I carried a bouquet for the hostess, the children had their extra sweaters and Jack brought his violin which we were all surprised to see when he pulled it from behind the driver's side seat. Our host, Max, had everything under control although it was going to be more than three hours before we sat down to dinner. Max was drinking a beer - one of many that night. He seemed totally at home and exuded confidence around his impressive cooking-channel type stove with pots boiling, grills spitting in a warm kitchen filled with the smells of garlic and basil, homemade baguettes and fresh pasta, sausage and red sauce. I liked talking to Max so I settled onto a stool with a good view of the chef in action. Vanessa, our hostess, was too much for me - too tall, too wide, too loud, too busty, too affectionate, too perfumed, too red in the lipstick department and too in love with my husband. She and Jack wandered to her backyard.

I didn't put it all together that night, but it was definitely odd. The seating arrangements around the dinner table grouped the children in the middle, Max and me at one common corner of the table and Vanessa and Jack next to each other at the other end. Don't try to picture it, it was uneven - an uneven distribution of people, chairs and space. Vanessa poured red and white wine for herself. Max had another beer, Jack and I had sparkling water, and the children had soda. Dinner was great and everyone enjoyed eating because we were starving, for starters, and also because it was delicious. Everyone, except Vanessa, that is, who spent her entire time taking pictures of everyone around the table. At one point she said, snapping away, "You don't mind if I take some pictures of your husband, do you?"

"No," I answered, not ever having been asked that question and trying to be a gracious guest. So, she did - all angles, close-ups, head shots, leaning in, then out, and with direction, "Look up, good, Now look over here, and look down, and with a smile. Now, no smile. Great - yummy."

"Yummy?" I muttered.

After dinner Vanessa organized a "concert" featuring her younger daughter, eight-year-old, Nancy, playing her child size violin, only to be followed by a piece Vanessa requested of Jack. When Jack agreed to play, Vanessa was undone. It was if we were heading to Florence for the concert of the century.

Max and I, and the other children applauded appropriately for Nancy, "Good job! That was beautiful. Thank you so much, Nancy. That was just great!" And then struggled to try and find something appropriate to say for Jack, a 42-year-old man who played a song with a similar degree of difficulty while Vanessa swooned as if she needed smelling salts to stay with the intensity of her evening.

When we finally headed out the door at 10:30, I was exhausted and spinning. What the heck had gone down there? As the children fell asleep on the way home in the back seat, Jack and I talked about the evening and the relationship between Max and Vanessa, while I completely missed the obvious. The relationship that had interesting discussion potential belonged to my husband and Vanessa.

Two weeks later the dam broke, the shit hit the fan, and the fat lady sang. Jack and Vanessa were busted the night Max drove to the Decathlon Club at 2:00 A.M. when Vanessa didn't come home. Seeing his wife's car and Jack's truck next to each other in the parking lot outside of one of the club's hotel rooms, Max knocked on the door to be greeted by his naked wife while Jack called from the bed in the distance, "Who is it?" As Max told the story to me, he was seething when he spit at Vanessa, "Get home," turned on his heel and left because if he had stayed, he would have killed him - Jack, that is.

The crazy thing about it all was that we two couples were running down our individual paths of destruction in parallel except that the only ones who knew the whole story were Jack and Vanessa. Max didn't call me when he found them at their Decathlon sleepover. I was busy packing to move to the North Shore and keep our appointments with Lutheran Brotherhood whose counselors were meeting with us separately to help Jack address his sex addiction and keep me focused on our finances. As the clock was counting down, Jack and I were on our last days together as a couple and our last times together as a family, but I didn't know that. I was frankly very frustrated with Jack who insisted that we have a getaway night for ourselves before I started driving up North. He was staying back to finish up his last karate classes, so we'd be apart for a week or so.

"Sweetness, call your parents and see if William and Molly can stay with them this Saturday night so we can go out for dinner and have a night to ourselves. I can drop them off if you need to keep packing, and we could get them by noon Sunday. We need some time together. This has been a rough couple of weeks."

We had been in therapy less than a month, in couple/separate/ and now what turned out to be our last couple configuration during which Jack admitted that he was having an affair with Vanessa, but "it isn't much. It just happened." As a result, he was given an assignment to tell Vanessa within 24 hours that it was over, to which he agreed. Jack also admitted to an active life of pornography online in our home. His assignment was to follow specific instructions with me present to "lock himself out" and set up control of our computer under a password that only I knew. He agreed to that also and we committed to taking action when we got home that same day. All of this came out in one session during which both our therapists were present. At the end, there were four people, focused, listening, all eyes focused on the male therapist who summed it up,

"This is fundamental. It is basic. You have quite a road ahead of you that will require commitment and tenacity from you both if you want to keep your marriage and your family intact. If these two commitments are met, we can look at moving forward, if not, your life together is most likely over - as you, Annie, have said you will not live with either of these conditions."

So, at the same time Jack was negotiating for a getaway night at, you got it, The Decathlon Club, my response was,

"Wait a minute, are you going to tell Vanessa that it is over with you? And when is that going to happen? And my parents don't like spur of the moment anything plus they are not into sleepovers. This just isn't a good idea and there is just too much to do to finish the school year and pack and get on the road. Let's wait until we get up North."

"I'll take care of Vanessa. I'll tell her tonight. I need you, Annie. Your mom loves to have time with William and Molly, and she'll understand. It's just one night. I'll take care of everything, no need to pack a thing - just meet me - come with me." And then his hands took my hands. I was out of arguing. I didn't know what to think. I wanted to escape or better yet return to denial, but there were too many new facts out now. I just wanted to be loved, secure, one man, one woman, no crazy side shows. I loved our little family. I loved Jack. And then with a big sigh, I heard myself say,

"Alright, I'll call my mom."

I cannot describe most lovemaking in my life. By that I mean, what exactly was going on or what I was thinking, but the very strange thing is that there are two times in my life where I can. Once, when I came back from Africa having climbed Kilimanjaro. Jack met me at the airport and brought me home. We couldn't make love because he had a Herpes outbreak, but we masturbated together in the moonlight that shone in the bay window onto our bedroom floor. That was hot. The second was our getaway night at the Decathlon Club.

We had dinner somewhere that I cannot remember, nor do I remember anything about the day and the children, or any drama required for pulling this evening off. What I do remember is an uninteresting room with a double bed, an adequate bathroom, our clothes draped over chairs, and the two of us, clean, warm and naked in between the sheets. I wanted Jack. He had called me earlier in the day to say he talked to Vanessa. So, I knew that, but how that manifested itself in my body and in my desire was new to me. I was hot and horny, wanting my husband, to kiss him, to take all the time in the world to turn him on, to respond with my hands and my mouth, to stroke, feel and taste with more intensity than I had known. I was the pursuer and this night I wanted my husband deliriously satisfied more than I wanted my own sweet exhaustion. This was the only time in my life that I got lost in my enjoyment of giving oral sex. It was like I was awake, not ashamed, not unsure of myself, but rather free, ready to devour and tantalize that beautiful penis, that man who was mine and who I was reclaiming. It was a time of self-assuredness sexually. I loved being in bed with Jack that night not only because he loved it but because I went everywhere I wanted to go and held back nothing. When we were lying with our heads on the pillows, talking afterwards, I asked Jack,

"What did Vanessa say when you told her it was over?"

"She cried," he answered. Then it was quiet, our bodies still, touching here and there because of how we were lying. I pulled up the top sheet when I started to feel chilled, thinking we might drop off to sleep any moment, peaceful and secure in our connection.

Then Jack spoke again, "Do you want to know what I was really thinking through all of this?" Jack spoke quietly."

"What?" I asked.

"How, after all this time and everything we have been through and tried, and how far we have come …what that would be like to start all over again."

"You mean….sexually?" Honestly, I didn't have to ask. My heart sank before he replied, "Yeah." And then he laughed.

That was the moment when not all the pieces had found their way to each other, but they were coming into the light. I thought we were still a couple, but I didn't know what that meant. There was an ugliness to being in the presence of a predator and having been used again. I understood on some level that I was with someone who only wanted sex and a free ride. Our children and a life rich with experiences were by products that didn't matter. I loved our family. I felt so alone with what I thought was a narrow escape from our family breaking apart that I couldn't fathom that the only thing that occurred to Jack to say was that there was a long road ahead to groom his next victim. I knew it from the laugh, it was all a game to him.

Chapter 9
A Day at a Time

Aaaah life in the Corporate World. Little did I know how valuable all those Management 101 skills would be. For eighteen years I had been a trainer for Honeywell, on the front lines in classes around the country hammering home Theory X and Theory Y Management, MacGregor's <u>The Human Side of Enterprise</u>, the Myers-Briggs Instrument, passionately teaching skills in which I believed and practiced myself.

I knew all about author Stephen Covey. I owned his planner. I was a follower of his philosophy as laid out in his best seller, <u>The Seven Habits of Highly Effective People.</u> Begin with the end in mind. Seek first to understand then to be understood.

In addition to that I had AA running through me. "First things First. Take It Easy. One Day at a Time." *and* I had been raised on "This is the day that the Lord hath made. Let us rejoice and be glad in it."

It wasn't that I was acutely aware of all I had learned when my life fell apart, or that I deliberately set about doing what I had enthusiastically taught for twenty years. Clearly, I was *not* thinking in terms of prioritized lists of goals for the day, week, month and year with Gant charts, timetables and portable checklists to monitor accountability. No no no. I was just showing up each day, at the long, rough-hewn table in the cabin, breathing in the early hours of another surrealistic morning before William and Molly woke up, reaching for my Stephen Covey planner because that's what I knew to do. I had a yellow Papermate pencil that I held and didn't use, at least for a while, because what I looked at every morning was just so exquisite. It captivated me.

Out our floor-to-ceiling picture windows that made up the walls of our cabin on three sides, to the right and to the left as far as you could see, was Her Majesty, Lake Superior. Her shoreline headed for Canada to the north and Duluth to the south. Away across her waters, barely discernible some days, was Wisconsin, and just below in the foreground, the North Star Island.

If you know Walt Disney's movie, "Peter Pan" and the famous views of Never Never Land when Peter flies Wendy, John and Michael toward their new home, then you know our view of North Star Island. In the mist, it was identical, surrounded by crashing waves on the side open to the sea and calm on the opposite side, revealing rocks and trees as the fog moved in and away, eagles caught in the updrafts soaring overhead, accompanied by seagulls crying out in their unmistakable, "Caw Caw."

Her Majesty, Lake Superior, was mesmerizing. Every day. Vast and powerful. Every day. Mysterious and unpredictable or peaceful and hypnotic. Even when She was hidden because the fog was so thick. She was a magnificent presence. Every day.

And so each morning I would sit, entranced. Sometimes my eyes rested on the smallest movement of a blade of grass near to me, as it walked with the wind. More often, my gaze landed on the water and stayed there, watching a whitecap form and disappear or noticing the deep gray of the cold, cold water changing its hue according to the sky and clouds above. While my eyes rested, so did my pencil, poised to be effective, efficient, productive, but never hurrying me from that time when I took it all in and was reminded that God was good. "All was well and all would be well." I recalled from the writings of Julianne of Norwich, theologian and mystic of the 13th century.

I had happened onto an amazing combination for beating the odds of impending doom. Begin with an early morning dose of sensory saturation: beauty, magnificence, power to wake up my Type A brain that was comfortable on autopilot when it came to problem solving and achievement. Add energy, which I happened to be blessed with in abundance. Dust with a touch of fear, and I was ready for the day. My reality became irrelevant. It simply couldn't matter. I put my pencil on the calendar page, sure there was a plan for us. It was just a matter of finding it. And so, the lists, the priorities, the problem solving began.

Okay. So, let's see. So far, we knew some faces in Two Harbors, we had a repaired lawn mower on the way, I had an AA group to go to every Friday and Monday nights, and we were chipping away at the Box Mountain. I had called the people whom I thought should know about our turn of events. It was a short list: my two oldest sons, my two brothers, my sister, my mom and stepdad. The collective response was, "Oh, Annie, we are so sorry. What happened? How? We're so so sorry. We love you. We know you can beat this. You'll be alright."

I loved that my oldest boys wanted to take Jack out. "Just say the word, Mom; we know people who know people who know people. You don't even have to know."

I loved that my siblings did what they could. Robby, next in birth order, sent me $1000 with the note, "For every birthday I missed and for all to come."

Charlie, third in line, spent hours on the phone with me applying his lawyer skills to property, child protection and divorce issues. He also hired me on a regular basis to do ridiculous tasks for him at his cabin which was just two miles down the road.

"Hey, Annie, I hate to bother you because I know you've got your hands full. But I was wondering if I could hire you to help me out."

He actually paid me $50 to check a leaking hot water heater, and $75 to turn off the water main under his cabin so his pipes wouldn't freeze. He bought my canoe for $500 - said he'd been looking for one to have Up North. He kept a little money coming my way, loaned me a $1400 chunk and never said no when I called to sort out my predicaments. In another time, I would have turned water on and off, checked pipes and loaned Charlie my canoe as a normal part of being his sister in a family that was raised on helping each other. But these days, I was scraping together pennies to make it day to day, and I was grateful for the money. Even when I responded to Charlie's requests, "Hey, sure you *can* hire me, but I'd be glad to run down…you don't have to pay me," he was ready and convincing with, "Listen, I know I don't have to; but this really saves me a royal pain-in-the-ass drive up north just to take care of the change of season's minutia. I just don't have the time and if you could do it, you'd be doing me a huge favor. I'm going to pay someone to take care of the place so I'm paying anyway. Is 75 bucks enough?"

"$75 would be great." I responded. "Sure. Thanks a lot."

"Hey, no, thank *you*!" Charlie said as he signed off without a hint of pity in his voice.

In August that summer my brother Robby and his family made their annual trip from Massachusetts to Minnesota to see everyone. Robby, an artist, musician and professional carpenter, always made it a working vacation and this year helped my mom and stepdad, Beryl, with decking and roofing projects. My parents owned two cabins right next to each other, the main cabin, and a smaller, more rustic guest cabin which they had sold to Charlie. When Charlie and his family drove up from St. Paul to visit and lend a hand, I had the rare opportunity to be with both my younger brothers at the same time.

The last morning before Rob was going back east, I asked the boys if they could come up for a little while. I was aching for the roots of our family, for feeling surrounded, for some protection. I really missed my dad. They walked in the front door of my cabin laughing at something stupid between the two of them which always cracked me up. Then one of them must have nudged the other because they straightened up as if to acknowledge that my situation was serious and maybe they should have more of a funeral-type demeanor like someone died here.

"I just wanted some time with you, to lean on you and gather some strength from being with you," I started. "I could use a hug."

"Okay. Well sure. Alright, here you go," laughed Robby. We were generally the same height for hugging purposes, 5'5" - 5'8," but Robby was three times as thick as me and all muscle, an example of having used his whole body, especially his hands to create and build all his life. He put his strong arms around me in a sort of awkward way and gave me a big squeeze. I was happy.

Charlie, taller and also muscular, was built like my dad with his barrel chest and resemblance to my dad's facial features. Charlie looked put together, like a lawyer, and watched the hug, probably figuring Rob took care of that. I knew one hug spoke for both of them.

"Would you like to go for a short hike? Up the Jeep Trail?" I asked.

"Sure," they both answered. Out we went, climbing the short hill behind our cabin to get on the wide, grassy path which led to the trail system that wove in and about the North Star property. We had plenty of room to walk three across, me in the middle of two twice as wide and half again as tall gentlemen, my brothers.

"What do you think Dad would have said about all this?" I asked as we walked by the handmade log bench overlooking North Star Island.

"You mean, about Jack?" asked Charlie.

"Yeah…about the whole thing that has happened to me." I answered.

I can't exactly remember what they piped in, but it had a "Jesus H. Christ! What a goddamn mess!" in it; adding that Dad wouldn't have been too pleased and that he would have handled it. I took that to mean handled Jack and taken care of his little girl. I liked the sound of that. Oh, how I longed for someone to swoop in and take care of this, of me, the children, all of it.

"I think Dad would be really proud of you," said Robby.

"Yeah, you're doing all the right things, Annie," added Charlie, "You are figuring it out. You'll get there."

It was something like that. It didn't really matter, the exact words. What did matter was being sandwiched between them for a little while, feeling the father I missed so much, allowing me the luxury of leaning. I could take a breather.

I kept my spot between them as we walked, linking arms as if on the Yellow Brick Road. We laughed about our high school production of "The Wizard of Oz," in which Robby had been a munchkin, forced to try out by Dad who insisted that learning to dance would make him a better wrestler. Robby hated every minute of it, although he was a very convincing Munchkin. Meanwhile, I brought the house down as the Wicked Witch of the West. After a chorus of "We're off to see the Wizard" including the "move on down the road" footwork, we chattered about all our lives, kids, their wives, work, school.

In that time, I was clearly reminded that I was okay. They cared about me; I could see that. They believed in me. After all, I was the oldest. I had a track record for coming through; and while they curbed their goofiness to some extent, the fact that they were who they always were around each other, was calming, comforting and restorative. It was a touch point to a place in a time more familiar than the chaos of the last couple months…a touch point that reminded me that if anyone here could get something done, it was me. No one said those words that day, but they behaved like they thought so. And so, I thought so, too.

And finally, my sister, Claire, the baby of the family, younger than me by eight years, called to announce, "I am going to call you every couple of days to make sure you are alright." And she did. She never let go. She became the person with whom I was the most open about money. I couldn't support us. I didn't have enough. She stayed right with me over the next 6 years, providing loans totaling $9000, loaned in thousand-dollar chunks - paid back, borrowed again, paid back again - until I finally paid it all back with interest and stood on my own two feet.

As for my mom, Betty, and her 2nd husband of 20 years, Beryl, I learned the painful truth that they were not available. They had a lot of money, millions. Mom had married Beryl after ten years on her own, following my dad's early death from pancreatic cancer at age 46. Beryl looked good - at a distance - a little stuffy, and certainly not the amazing, larger-than-life man my father had been. Beryl was a prominent doctor in the Twin Cities, and former neighbor of ours in Sunfish Lake Village. I don't know why he set his sights on Mom, because we McMillans did not come from the club of the private school elite, and it seemed like those pedigrees set boundaries in Sunfish Lake that weren't crossed. I was well aware that some Sunfish Lakers thought you should know your place, even though your place was just fine and their obsession with status was silly. Nevertheless, the unspoken rules were out there.

Betty McMillan was a catch, no doubt about it. Beryl's wife had also died of cancer so maybe it just all came together because of proximity in the neighborhood. I stopped trying to understand the dance Mom and Beryl were doing when I learned to stop going home to Mom for support during my early days of sobriety. My AA sponsor agreed that my instincts for my mother's support were right and good. My mom just wasn't going to be able to be there for me. So I painfully moved on to find other wise women in whom to confide, and kept my relationship with my mom to safe topics: the weather, the children's activities and her travels with Beryl to the elder hostels of the world.

I don't harbor any resentment toward my mom. I loved her. I have the deepest respect for her. I have imagined that she knew better than anyone the kind of loss I was experiencing and that she wanted to be there for me just like her mother had held her together after my dad died. But she wasn't free. I will never fully appreciate the amount of energy she expended to survive her choice to marry and stay married to Beryl.

Maybe in another family people would have rushed to Two Harbors to be with me. It sometimes seemed to me that *someone* should drop what they were doing and just get there! But that didn't happen. I didn't ask for that and I clearly never entertained moving so I could be closer to someone in my family. I was really on my own. More importantly, I now see how deeply comfortable, how peaceful I was in choosing to be on my own. Because you know what? I wasn't.

I was my father's daughter, tough, tenacious, irreverent, and not interested in being encumbered by another person who couldn't keep up. I was willing to walk spiritually in complete faith that God and Her Majesty had the plan. I let go of my fear, my need to know what was going to happen, the details of everything we didn't have. I knew my dad had his hand on my shoulder, and I knew that with every breath I took this was my time to use the extra I had been given because I had a few more precious conversations, days, experiences with my dad, simply by virtue of being the oldest.

When I witnessed racism as a ten-year-old on a trip to Atlanta, or when I couldn't compete because I was a girl, or when I took on the assistant minister in communicants class because Jesus said, "The only way to the Father is through me," which therefore, meant all the good people in the world who simply weren't exposed to Jesus Christ, were going hell, I complained bitterly to my dad, tears of frustration flowing, "That's not fair!"

Except for the minister and the communicants class injustice to which my dad replied, "He's an idiot," my father's responses to my questions were thoughtful and substantial. I felt heard. He took me seriously and gave me other ways to frame my frustrations, to see that I always had choices in what I *could* do. He also made me laugh, and I began my lifelong appreciation of the humor in the human condition.

Regarding the dumbed-down game of girls' basketball and the restrictions that prevented me from playing as hard as I could, I repeated my refrain, "It's just not fair!"

"That's the story my life, baby," Dad began, not in a self-serving way, but as an introduction to his life's story in which he accepted the hand he was dealt and went on to determine his own destiny rooted in a deep faith, and his belief in the power of love and hard work. When he would pick me up from school after cheerleading practice, the fifteen-minute drive home was rarely enough time to talk so we often sat in the driveway for a few extra minutes before we went in for dinner. I learned through his stories to value my freedom, to think for myself, to step out boldly in faith, to try anything, and to get up and try again if I stumbled or failed. I learned that he would do anything for me no matter how silly if it was important to me, like follow a script I wrote for him the night my high school crush was coming to pick me up for a date. I learned what it was like to have someone believe in me and delight in my accomplishments.

"You can swim across that lake, Annie," Dad said out of the blue the first time he and Mom brought our family to see the new property where our house would be built." Hornbeam Lake looked huge to me at 11 years old."

"I can?" I remember answering, totally surprised at the idea.

"Sure," Dad answered without hesitation, "I'll go with you. Jump into your suit, and I'll meet you at the shore.

Dad had taught me the crawl, taking a breath after four strokes rather than two. He also taught me to flip over into a back stroke if I got tired or to finish a swim off with a relaxed breaststroke, so although I thought the lake looked very big, I wasn't afraid of drowning.

We did swim that lake, probably twice the distance across because I zig zagged so much when I was in backstroke mode. There was no chit chat, but Dad was there, swimming near enough to me if I had gotten in trouble. I looked once, saw him out of the corner of my eye and then got back to my job of swimming.

"Good for you, I knew you could do it. I'm proud of you, Annie," Dad said as we reached the shore.

That was the same year Dad taught me to drive on the dirt road that wound around from the ten cabins to the fish house at Sve's Split Rock Cabins - another unexpected vote of confidence that added to the feeling that I could do anything. He taught me to see things in new perspectives, to tell the truth, and he let the consequences do the teaching. On a summer night at sixteen, I came home late having been stopped by our local policeman for driving a golf cart with my friends around and around in the alfalfa fields. My dad's response was, "Glad you are home safely. It sounds like you learned something tonight. See you in the morning, honey."

Life was for living with gusto. Interest and curiosity about others, listening, finding the good, having fun, cheering the effort and finding ways to be of service made for a good life. I had proof of that. My parents were in sync no matter what came their way. Their messages were clear, and I considered myself the lucky one to have been given so much before my dad died.

There was peace as I started my days in the cabin. Planning what to do was without struggle because I believed the power that awaited me would be more than I needed. I suppose that kind of faith would seem to some like flying blind. Not to me. I was flying with my eyes wide-open making a deliberate daily choice. I liked being on my own at the long, rough-hewn table in the cabin each day, greeting Lake Superior and planning the day's adventures that would move us down the road.

Chapter 10
Seagull Friends

It was of utmost importance to act with confidence when presenting solutions to the problems posed by William and Molly. Quick answers and good posture suggested security and stability. A smile and a well enunciated plan…any plan… suggested that I knew what I was doing. Solutions that were beyond what an eight and three-year-old could conjure up, spoken with enthusiasm and a wide-eyed look of wonder, entertained and kept them coming back for more, slowly replacing fear, sadness and despair with enchantment, fun and hope. As long as I was committed to the next great idea and excited about getting us out of our various predicaments, I kept the big one at bay: Are you leaving too? When? What about us?

My commitment to the schemes to beat our challenges was what gave meaning to the core message, "We're going to be alright." And since our schemes were fun and always a little quirky, they were engaging for all of us and a lot more attractive than worry or pity as a way to spend the day.

For example, Molly excitedly announced in the midst of a Box Mountain Saturday, "I know what the problem is!" She looked as if she was ready to burst forth with the secret to life.

"What?" I asked, matching her enthusiasm.

"We need a dad."

My silence as I let that one settle, spurred her on. "Because, when you tuck William in then I don't have anyone to read to me and when you are with me then William doesn't have anyone." And then the heartbreaker, "Do you think Josh would be our dad too?"

Josh was my first husband, and the father of my two older boys, Oliver and Christopher, and a good man. To Molly and William, he was kind and friendly, a person with whom they crossed paths at summer softball tournaments. Quickly picking my battles, I went with Molly's first concern regarding bedtime and said,

"Molly, you are right! And I know just what to do about that! Let's make one big bed that belongs to the three of us - up in the loft - on the floor where we can each sleep side by side - each on our own futons with our own blankets and our own pillows - but right next to each other. I can sleep in the middle and hold each of your hands, and I can read to you both until it's time to close our eyes. And that way no one will have to be alone at night at bedtime. Do you think you could help me, and we could try it tonight?"

"No problem...we'll do *this*!" or "Here's our plan on *that*!" or even "Well now, that's a good one! I don't know, but I know who does!" all spoken with a cheery disposition, got us a long way. Thank God I was a glass-half-full kind of girl. I never had to work at seeing the possibilities, and that was what we needed, a pile of possibilities to sort through the same way we sorted through possible agates on the beach.

It didn't take me long to get the rhythm of leading with confidence. In the children's silences I'd sense a question or complaint soon to be spoken. I relaxed into what they had to say, listening carefully and only asking questions for clarification. With a little back and forth, we could agree on the problem and bingo! I would answer them and solve the problem. Answer however!! Didn't have to consult, didn't have to check with anyone else, as in husband or "your father." Just answer their question and get on with it. It was *all* up to me, and it was all up to *me*! I liked this. It was efficient and easy, and I made great decisions. And even when I didn't now and then, I'd just make another decision.

When William said, "We don't have any friends," at the end of a particularly long day of introducing ourselves to Two Harbors, I opted for,

"Of course we do. I'll show you!" rather than, "Are you kidding? What do you expect? We just moved here and what do you think we've been doing all day? We're making friends. Or at least we're trying. But, it takes a while."

"It's okay here," William continued from the back seat, "but, Mom, we just don't have any friends."

"Yeah," piped in Molly, straining to see out her window as Flood Bay sped by.

Flood Bay was a small wayside beach north of Two Harbors on our drive home. The waves crashed there. I always liked that little spot because you could just see enough from the highway through the trees and tall grass, to the white caps and what the seagulls were up to.

I heard William. I heard Molly's, "Yeah." I saw Flood Bay out of the corner of my eye, and I was already mentally counting the money in my pocket, my mind set on the large size bag of Old Dutch popcorn which I was pretty sure cost $3.19 three miles back at the Holiday station.

I pulled a u-ie as soon as the road dipped, and I could see that oncoming traffic was way off in the distance. In minutes we were at the Holiday station. In a couple more minutes we were out of there. I had the popcorn and a large bottle of Frosty root beer for us all to share as we headed back to Flood Bay. We pulled into the parking lot and hopped out into the wind. Looking down the shore to the cliffs along the beach, we saw a few lone seagulls, circling slowly, catching an up draft, then heading for the water.

"William, Molly come grab a handful of popcorn to eat and another handful to throw," I said heading for the water as I opened the bag of popcorn.

"Here, have some more," I added as I threw my handfuls as high as I could into the wind. By the third handful thrown whimsically into the air, we had friends... three, then four, then a half dozen... seagulls, gliding in, landing right at our feet, eagerly pecking at our popcorn. Another round of handfuls into the air and a dozen more of their seagull friends flew in to join the party. By the end of the bag we were *surrounded* by 50 birds, squawking, flapping, a little preening and finally flying off for the cliffs in the distance.

We stood on an empty beach, just the three of us, an empty bag of popcorn in one hand, other little hands passing root beer back and forth. I looked at the children. I looked at the seagulls away far away by now and ran to climb on top of the nearest big boulder shouting into the wind, "We've got friends! Hey everybody! We've got some friends!"

William and Molly laughed and shouted too, jumping and waving hello and good-bye to our friends down the shore.

"Yeah!! We've got friends!! We've got seagull friends! Hey! Seagulls! Hello … Over here!! Good-bye. Good-bye for now" The children came climbing after me first to sit on the big rock and then into the car. "Wow!" said William, closing the door, "That was awesome!"

"I know!! And you know what?" I whispered as I leaned into the back seat to get near their faces, "I'm pretty sure…that… if we come back tomorrow… and the day after tomorrow… and the day after tomorrow's tomorrow… They'll be waiting for us!! What do you say?"

"Really? They will?" asked William, intrigued with this prediction. And after some pause, "Okay!"

"Can I throw the popcorn first next time?" asked Molly.

"Can I just be out there by myself with the seagulls?" countered William.

"How will they know it's us?"…and a million more questions and chatter all the way home about seagulls and friends and living on Lake Superior.

Chapter 11
An Angel Named Christine

As far back as I can remember Christmas; I have known that angels are big people – big in spirit and presence and goodness. But more than that, angels are tall and strong, energetic and handsome…. and men. I am sure of that because I saw them with my very own eyes when I sat in the second row pew at House of Hope Presbyterian Church at the age of five, in my red, boiled-wool coat, legs dangling because a five-year-old only has enough legs to dangle off an adult size pew. I saw the angels every year after that, too, sitting in that same pew on Christmas Eve, taking in the glory and wonder of the five o'clock Christmas Eve Service.

I was mesmerized the first time I saw the Motet choir process to "O Come All Ye Faithful" in their black robes and starched, white surplices, balancing their individual candles with their hymnals as they floated down the aisle and up the steps that wound around toward the balcony. I listened to the prophets read a dozen scriptures about the coming of the baby Jesus, fascinated by the spit that flew beyond their scraggly, glued on, men-of-the Bible beards as they enunciated their passages. Mr. Baker took the cake every year, "Wooooooooonnnnderful! Counnnnselor. The Mighty Gawwwwwd. The Everlasting Father. The Prrrrrrinnnnce of Peace." I sang all the Christmas carols because I had known them by heart by the time I was four. I smelled the incense of the We Three Kings, and, best of all, I saw the Angels. I loved the Angels!

The elegant program, scripted on linen-like paper the size of a large postcard, described The Christmas Eve Service at House of Hope as a pageant of music and tableaux depicting the advent and birth of the Christ child as painted by artists of the Renaissance. Its formality invited me then, and still does today, to sit a little taller and listen more attentively because I was in the presence of masterpieces, glorious music and God's story.

Each tableau was portrayed by members of the congregation, dressed and positioned exactly as the masterpiece painting itself. Those specially selected "actors" were quietly assembled behind an enormous black scrim at the top of the five steps that led into the chancel. As soon as Mrs. Zylpha Morton, creator and director gave the signal, the "painting" had to hold perfectly still for two minutes while spotlights from a distance went from no light to fully lit, then back to no light, bringing the majestic artwork to life for a minute. The beauty was in the reveal when not a sound could be heard except for the one lone cougher who couldn't hold it until the next carol or reading from the pulpit.

As soon as I heard our minister say the words, "…shepherds, watching over their flock by night," I knew we were almost to the Angels. "And Lo!" our minister continued, picking up the pace, "An angel of the Lord appeared with the heavenly host! And the glory of the Lord shone round about them, and they were sore afraid. 'Be not afraid' the angel said to them, 'I bring you glad tidings of a great joy that will be for all people.' Suddenly, a great company of the heavenly host appeared with the angel, praising God and saying, 'Glory to God in the highest and on earth peace, good will to man with whom he is well pleased.'"

Then, at that moment, the lights would slowly come up revealing three shepherds, each lying on the ground by the campfire, leaning back on one arm, elbows bent, while reaching up with the other arm to shield their faces from the brilliance of six dazzling angels. Draped in long, flowing flamingo-colored robes, tied at the waist with a thin white rope, they balanced at their mouth a long, shiny brass horn pointing toward the heavens… each at a slightly different height because they themselves were different heights or on various platforms behind the scrim, but all perfectly parallel save the newer cast members whose horns dipped a bit when they got a little wobbly at the end.

All in all, these were great looking angels! Handsome, curly haired, high school jocks clothed Da Vinci "Davids," with one larger-than-life angel standing behind and above them, arms outstretched like a magnificent eagle. Best of all, they were fully lit for an extra two minutes while the choir sang "Angels We have Heard on High." The painting is a Ruben. To my young eyes it was amazing.

Anyway, once I saw those angels, I was ready for them when they manifested themselves along the path of my life. And that's exactly what happened. I knew it the second or third time that I met Chistine. She was the same kind of awesome as the angels that first filled my heart on Christmas Eve as a little girl. Christine was tall; easily 5'10"; beautiful and powerful. She had broad shoulders, long legs, a huge smile, translucent skin without any make up, and medium length blond hair that was straight and shiny. She had great hands that did real work…like raising three children in a small house that was always filled with smells of the bread she baked and the soups she made.

Christine kept her kitchen cupboards stuffed with the best bargain sizes of all the staples, cereals and snacks that any organized homemaker would ever want. She had meal plans and shopping lists on display at eye level, coupon drawers and piles of booklets filled with stamps for the gas station. By her side door were hooks for all kinds of jackets, hats and mittens, while her cupboards and countertops were home to yogurt makers, a Mixmaster, wire whips, spatulas and every kind of pan, Jello mold and jar.

When school began in September, Molly and I eagerly made our daily trek from our car parked on the street to Christine's side door, which we opened ourselves as we sang, "Good morning, Christine." We paused for the slightest moment on the steps until we heard, "Good morning, Annie and Molly," which was our green light to step all the way into her warm and cozy kitchen crowded with day care kids and moms all jockeying for a little space to unload and say hello.

It was a room way too small for all of us each morning, but who cared? It was a place to be tucked in and held in a little community of like-minded moms and kids, filled with love that consisted of bending down, undressing and dressing, hugging and kissing, babbling and clucking… morning busy-ness that I loved, that I knew how to do, that made sense to me in a new world where not much else did. That time was so precious, so valuable, so unlike any other time in my day. And I cherished it. I recognized Christine. She wasn't a man, but I knew an angel was presiding in that kitchen; and I knew I was safe and secure in her presence and the presence of God.

Christine was the mom in the Lakeside neighborhood of Duluth that provided day care. She came out of nowhere, a suggestion from a mom I didn't know at the parents' meeting I attended when I was enrolling the children at St. Mark's Lakeside school, a private Catholic elementary school for families in St. Mark's parish.

"Hi, Christine," I began when I called her the next day, "My name is Annie Stewart. We haven't met but I am new in town; actually, I live north of Two Harbors. I was at the parents' meeting last night for St. Mark's where William, my third grader, will attend along with my daughter, Molly, who will be in the afternoon preschool class. We are an out-of-parish family, actually we are Presbyterian, but very excited about the school year. St. Mark's is our first choice."

"Well, that's great," replied Christine. "Welcome to the St. Mark's family."

"Thank you so much," I continued, "Anyway, Molly is eligible to attend the afternoon sessions only, so I need help every morning. A woman in the meeting last night called out, 'Try Christine.' when I asked about day care possibilities." Christine laughed in a warm, seemingly amused way as she replied,

"Unfortunately, I am full." And then before I could panic, she added, "Come on over anyway and we'll work something out."

For the next three years she did just that, allowing me to pay what and when I could at a reduced rate, accommodating a changing schedule as I tried to find interviews and work.

Christine was the place from which I set sail every day as I ventured out to rebuild a life for William, Molly, and me. Dropping William off at school and then taking Molly to Christine' s every morning was a pattern I liked. I liked being a player. I liked having something to say to her question, "What have you got going today, Annie?"

I always hung around after the other mothers hurried out the door to get to their jobs on time, just so I could describe my whole plan for the day, an important effort that kept me from discounting my seemingly small steps. The big "L" -- LOSER -- was waiting in the wings, but I found that she never made an entrance if I had a plan and fuel, both of which were replenished each day in Christine's kitchen.

"Today I am going to meet a person at McClaskeys who advertised some positions in the paper. Also, the principal of St. Mark's told me to check in with Father Tom about cleaning the parish kitchen. There might be work there. And I have my running shoes with me so I'll get a couple of miles in before I pick up Molly and William.

"That's a good day's work! Good for you, Annie. I'll put in a good word for you about the cleaning. We need someone, especially after the Friday Fish Frys."

"Oh, thank you, Christine," I said, feeling my spirits lift. "I have been cleaning since I was old enough to apprentice, shall we say. I learned from the best, my mother, and have been a professional since my college summer days. I will do an excellent job."

"I have no doubt. You are in my prayers, and I am already looking forward to hearing how it goes. Well, I've gotta get cooking - time for oatmeal and some fresh fruit. Annie, have a good day. Timmy, bring the rest of your friends to the table; time to wash up and have breakfast."

I did more to find work, get divorced, and get to the bottom of the demise of my former life because of Christine than I ever imagined I could. Mostly it wasn't pretty. I didn't care. If Woody Allen believed that 80% of life was showing up, that was good enough for me. I slapped on the best "fake it 'til you make it" face I could muster, grabbed a hold of a positive attitude and made sure that I had a plan every morning when I walked in the side door of Christine's.

Walking out and putting my plans into action? Well, that ranged from efforts that were totally feeble to some rather impressive activity. All days included the same lonely pit in my stomach, a feeling that was waiting for me when I stepped into the fresh air from Christine's kitchen. Taking the day's first steps toward something new, the conversation with myself would begin,

"Hey, everybody's got to start somewhere. Going for a run this early in the morning when you are fresh is really a bonus!! Someday when you have a job again you'll look back on this time and wish for the freedom and the time to stay in shape, so let's go for it...have a great two miler. Okay here we go."

Some days, I just couldn't. I'd go to the car and sit and stare or drive around the same five miles for the whole morning. Some days I would run, walk-run, then cry. Some days I had an interview. Some days I'd look through the paper for work. Whatever it was, that place in between friendship in Christine's kitchen and trying something new was always hard. But little by little I tolerated it and tried to accomplish something every day until low and behold, I had public assistance, a food shelf plan, clothes from Neighbor to Neighbor secondhand shop, a job trading tuition for cleaning the school, a way to start selling Weekenders Clothing, a bona fide divorce lawyer, and a variety of therapists holding us together.

One morning I arrived with Molly and hung out a little longer than usual just to talk to Christine while she made French toast for the breakfast eaters that day. I was wittering on about cleaning houses, cleaning the school, the parish kitchen once a month and that I was putting together some promotional flyers for my cleaning business. In the midst of it, Christine said, "You are the most amazing woman I know. I really admire you, Annie. You are persistent and determined and you always have a positive attitude. Every day you see the good in your life and you keep going. I watch you work hard. I see you believe in yourself. It is beautiful and I am so blessed to know you."

And I remember standing there and thinking, *"Really? Me?"*

Maybe those things were true. Maybe I really was going to make it out. I had forgotten to take time to hope, I was working so hard. I agreed that everything Christine said was what I wanted to be, I just didn't feel that what I was doing was big enough for those words. Maybe my efforts didn't feel big enough because there seemed to be equally as much time when I was stuck. Well, I say stuck now, but looking back, I was moving as fast as I could. I just didn't understand that devastating loss drops you in quicksand and nothing moves quickly. Working hard was more of an inside job than it was about producing tangible results. Gaining momentum was a concept that I seemed to remember from another life. Now it was a step at a time, a deliberate step at a time where speed at anything was illusive. I had my hands so full of trying to figure out how to survive, that I stopped thinking much about the quality of my life, my values or my beliefs.

I essentially dropped out of my friends' lives in the winters due to depression. I substituted brief encounters with another human for relationships, saying hello to another parent while waiting for Molly at preschool or thanking the checkout lady at the grocery store. I cried rivers. If it hadn't been for William and Molly who never ceased to bring me joy, to make me laugh, to look at me with complete trust, I think I may have folded. Even in the months where days of the blues would run together and I could see I was getting nowhere, my children reminded me why I was slogging away. I never sat back and just for the fun of it asked myself, "What would I do if I had nothing, and William and Molly were hungry?" No need. Why ask a hypothetical question when you are living it? Besides, I already knew part of the answer to that. Start every day in Christine's kitchen and don't quit. Go to AA, make lists, trust in God and breathe fresh air.

To this day I am blown away by Christine just as I am by my Dr. who sent me $50 in her Christmas card our first year, and Marlene who handed me $100 on her way out the door after an impromptu visit, with "Here Annie, you need this more than I do. We love you."

And my ex-husband, Josh, who sent $200 and a message with Christopher who came up over the holidays, "Here, give this to Mom." And Sarah and Andy, our neighbors who employed me and loved me and ooohed and aaahhhhed over our efforts. And Mary and Daniel, our friends from church, who took us out to dinner on my birthday and included $1000 in my birthday card. And the ladies at church who paid my way so I could attend their retreat. And Ted, the Assistant Foreman, who made us his project, driving up our hill daily to see that things were in order. And our dentist who let me pay him over two years while I was growing my cleaning business. And Ethelyn Andrews, who included us at holiday dinners and in her artistic pursuits, introducing me to people who eventually employed me. And Nora and Jon who sent me $5,000 to get a car that had tires with treads, brakes that worked and an intact body, i.e. one in which the children couldn't see the road we were driving on through holes here and there. There were so many Angels surrounding us, catching us just before we fell, making sure we had enough, offering support, encouragement and belief in our dreams that I will happily be paying it forward for the rest of my life.

I saw Christine not long ago at a school play when she represented the Drama Board at the start of the performance.

"Good evening, everyone. I am Christine Stauffer and honored tonight to speak for the Drama Board at St. Mark's. We are dedicating tonight's performance to Angela, our principal, who leads us every day in pursuing excellence as we work together to educate our children. Angela, you are a woman of faith, intellect and kindness and we thank God for you. Please everyone, join me in standing and thanking Angela with a round of applause." After a standing ovation graciously acknowledged by Angela, Christine continued, "Children and parent volunteers, I know you can hear me backstage, so here comes a big thank you to each and every one of you for all your hard work. We are so excited to see tonight's performance." More applause, hoots, and a few whistles.

"And now," Christine concluded as she raised her arms, "On with the show!" Christine stood there, as straight and tall and beautiful as the Angel I always knew she was. She lit up the room. We found each other afterwards for a little while, exchanging big hugs and question upon question about how things were going. When we paused to catch our breaths, she said, "I have been meaning to call you because I am thinking about changing careers and I'd really like to talk with you about it. You are my mentor, you know."

Once again, I found myself standing there, thinking, *"Really? Me?"*

"Okay! I would love that!" I responded as we settled on our plan: eight o'clock, Saturday morning, breakfast at the Vanilla Bean in Two Harbors. I had heard it in a movie, I think, but this time it was for real - *I* had a date with an Angel.

Chapter 12
The Wizard of Oz

POP! Then CRACKLE! Noises like it was the fourth of July, followed by a rising cloud of smoke…on a good night. That was my cue to enter stage right as the Wicked Witch of the West and scare the livin' daylights out of a stage full of munchkins. Oh, it was so good to be bad, to come through the smoke, bent forward at the waist, green bony arm and fingers outstretched, with a broom in my other hand, only to rise up in a cackle that started with a long high-pitched scream before it settled into tumbles of heh-heh-heh-heh-heh-heh-heh-heh-heh.

Even though I personally knew and had hugged every single munchkin in the play, *and* I was just William's and Molly's mom, those children were terrified for a moment, which meant so was every other child sitting on the edge of their seat at the Duluth Playhouse summer production of "The Wizard of Oz." Usually gasps, little shrieks and some whimpering could be heard, but by the time parents had comforted their children, the scene had moved on to Dorothy meeting the Scarecrow for the first time, and all was cheery again on the yellow brick road to Oz. I knew I was doing my job when I left them crying. I loved their reactions, but I also wanted to stop the show and let them see it was all pretend. Of course, I opted for scary and let their tears go because I knew their delight would be all the sweeter when I would melt an hour later to their cheers and enthusiastic applause.

"On a good night," meant that Tom and his pyrotechnics were on the same page. Half of the time that was true, while the other half of our performances my entrances were cued in a variety of ways. Some nights I heard a click, just a single click, and that was it. Some nights a click and a cloud. Some nights I heard the Pop and Crackle but saw no cloud. One night in a different scene, I was descending from the roof where I had threatened Dorothy and her merry band of the Lion, the Tin Man and the Scarecrow only to hear Tom whispering, "Ann! You're on fire!"

"Thanks!" I whispered over my shoulder, "That was fun tonight."

"No, hurry! You're really on fire!" came more whispering.

"Yah, thanks I heard you and I appreciate it. I'm coming," I whispered back, thinking, *"Hold your horses. It's hard to hold a broom and a ton of costume and descend backwards with only one hand holding the ladder…in the dark!"*

As soon as I was within arms' reach, Tom and another stagehand pulled me down and wrapped me in a blanket to put out the fire that I thought was a compliment. No one got hurt in the dark silence of our backstage, and more importantly at that moment, my costume accommodated the uneven loss of a layer of skirt without a problem for the rest of the show.

"Thanks, you guys, thanks. I get it now, Tom! What happened?"

"Well, you really were great. I meant that too, but there was fire on the roof, and I couldn't get to it and then you were standing kind of on it. I'm really sorry. I don't know what exactly went wrong. But, I'll fix it."

Wardrobe had a new little project as did Tom, whose project was not as new as it was ongoing. But that's the thing about community theater where almost everyone is a volunteer. Tom was doing the best he could. Like the rest of us, he took direction and tried again, all with a smile on his face. So, I shrugged it off with "the show must go on" attitude and just hoped that more often than not I would appear with all three: Pop! Crackle! And smoke, not fire. Well aware that my hope was completely out of my control, I always had my cackle ready to make my entrances.

Interestingly enough, my cackle became something Molly thought was worth showing off when she made a new friend or sometimes when I came to pick her up.

"Mom, cackle! Will you please cackle?"

Happy to oblige I would take deep breath and bust up a peaceful gathering with a long, loud cackle followed by, "Weeeellll, my pretty. Who are you and is this your little dog, Toto?" Somewhere in Molly's conversation that day, "The Wizard of Oz" must have come up and I was glad she wanted to trot me and my cackle out again in some fashion. For all three of us, that first play and a dozen more over the next five years, launched wonderful experiences for us with other families in Duluth. Acting introduced us to new directors, new performance venues and new volunteer opportunities. We made lots of friends from lots of places which was just what we needed when we were new in town.

It was always a magical day at the Co-op grocery store when I would run into Katie who played Glinda, the Good Witch of the East. We could catch up and have a few laughs about our do-over moments on stage and how much we missed "Aaaaaaaaand we're ACTING" for Claude, our guest director from the west coast. That friendship is one of my most treasured.

Katie became a playwright and director. She cast me in the first play she wrote as the mother to her main character, an eight-year-old Jewish boy who had escaped on a ship to America. It was a true story which Katie had us rehearse and perform in a small black box theater space in Duluth to which she invited a select few for her directorial debut. One of her guests was the boy, now 85 years old, about whose story she had written. After the performance I met him. He came up close to me and grasped my hands with tears running down his cheeks.

"You were just like my mother," he spoke as he looked directly into my eyes.

"I thought you were her. You sang just like she did. I never saw her again after she put me on that steamer. I just can't believe it. Thank you, I think you were her," he finished and then stood for a while longer holding my hands. I held on too, and didn't move, except to lean forward and whisper, "Thank you. It was an honor to play your mother. Thank you."

I was confident that community theater could be a great place for William, Molly and I to make friends in the early days. Drawing on my experience I knew many people cast in a play often didn't know each other. I was sure we would meet others with the same desire to connect. Furthermore, my theater friends from as far back as I could remember had been looking for a place to just be who they were - and then be someone else, to have the fun of telling a story, dressing up, singing, and being in a community family that brought joy to others and a feeling of personal accomplishment.

I saw those things happen for William and Molly who were always so glad to be in another play with old friends, and eager to reach out to kids and adults they hadn't met. They learned to audition in spite of their fear, they learned to accept big and small parts, they learned how to follow direction, bringing characters to life in "Charlotte's Web, "'Charlie and the Chocolate Factory," "Annie," "The Weavers," and "Cats" which launched Molly's triple threat capability. It was after the lead in "Cats" talked with me about training Molly's voice in addition to ballet and theater, that Molly began lighting up the stage as the Witch in "Into the Woods," and as Adelaide in "Guys and Dolls." Her college scholarships were equally given by the theater, dance and voice departments. She discovered her talents and a great love for the arts; all of it beginning with auditions for "The Wizard of Oz."

On that point, that audition wasn't easy. They never are. I was a nervous wreck on the inside, even though I had played the Wicked Witch of the West in high school. The children were open to trying something together so I sucked it up and tried not to show how awkward and out of it I really felt signing in, not knowing a soul, and grabbing the half sheet pieces of paper full of dialogue with which we were expected to audition when our names were called.

"Yes, thank you. Great!" said Claude, after I had said my name was Annie Stewart and, on his cue, "Aaaaaaaaand we're ACTING!" had thrown myself into a super hideous voice and cackle plus my lines.

"I want to give you a correction," he responded. "Make this witch a little more nuanced with an agenda; a crafty, sneaky, clever, sly witch. Understood?" And when I nodded, I was off again at, "Aaaaaaaaaand we're ACTING!" trying to do something different that was more than full frontal witch.

"Very good," said Claude, "I like how you took that correction. Anything else?"

"Yes," I said, realizing I was in full view with all eyes on me in the large audition room lined with cross-legged people who were waiting to be called.

"I have two very talented children who I hope will be cast because we would need to be in this together, if I am cast. I would love this part and I just wanted you to know that."

"Okay. Thank you. Let's meet the kids."

Five-year-old Molly went first and sang, "Somewhere Over the Rainbow," during which Claude cut her off and said, "She's great and I don't care if she was not. She's so adorable, I have to cast her. Munchkin! And who is next?"

William stepped up and sang an animated version of "We're off to see the Wizard" which secured him three parts: a palace guard, a flying monkey and a senior munchkin. We were in! We got parts! And so began an experience with a schedule, different parts for us to learn, rehearsals that we all attended though we saw little of each other in the early stages of learning our parts off and on stage. And then the fun of performing, the applause, the curtain calls, greeting the audience in the lobby after we ran out the back of the theater, around to the front and in through the main entrance before the first people exited. Everything about it filled a big hole with happiness and success.

I have a slide show that a cast member made for us all using photos and short clips she gathered from auditions, to backstage life to the final curtain. She set it to "Somewhere Over the Rainbow" sung by Israel "IZ" Kamakawiwoole as he accompanies himself on his ukulele. In it, the short videos of William and Molly singing their hearts out, and me at my cackling best, alone in the theater at the front of the stage during a sound check, is what I hold in my heart as sheer, reach to the heavens joy. I feel that rush of happiness whenever I remember those days.

William and Molly have credited their theater experiences with their ease in presenting during college and on their jobs, and, of course, I am glad for that. They jump in. They participate. They are comfortable thinking on their feet. Moreover, they have a beautiful quality of knowing when not to take themselves too seriously. At the time of their growing up, the theater was a place where we could immerse ourselves in telling a story that was so much better than our own on the days that it was hard to take. Going where there was laughter, where there was affirmation, where there were other kids and parents having fun was essential for us. We were richly rewarded in a karma sort of way. We entertained and enchanted many audiences with our antics and our characters at the same time they filled us up with their standing ovations and their love.

Chapter 13
Sex

The change from active and willing wife of a sex addict to single mother of two children, on my own in the Northwoods, brought with it its own loss that emerged subtlety and slowly. I didn't see it coming; not that I had time to think about sex or notice I was feeling horny. Nevertheless, sometime in that first year, I noticed the pace of my life had slowed from hair on fire running scared to just running. I was calm, more relaxed, fully aware of choosing faith over fear, but more than that, there was breathing room and no fire to extinguish. I was awake with enough energy to ask myself,

"And how are you doing?" On this particular day I must have seen, read or heard something steamy because I made a plan to masturbate - to have a little date with myself when the children were gone, and I had nothing calling for my attention. Monday seemed perfect - just a weekend away.

I am writing this in my story because it is true, but I never would have said these words out loud or discussed feeling horny and what my plans were. That just wasn't part of my generation's girl talk, or any person talk, as far as I knew. I thought orgasms were great, I loved sex and a good romp in the hay, before, during and after - all of it - and I was willing to try anything... pretty much. Still, there was something private about love making to the point that it was embarrassing to put words to the feelings. I don't think I've ever even said the word "erotica," as if anyone would care.

When I did summon the courage to talk to my first husband, Josh, about doing something racy like, "How about we buy a cheap, dirty, paperback novel (which I actually already had in my possession from a shopping trip in the airport five minutes earlier) to read to each other on this long overdue getaway to Barbados?" I was met with a look as if I had said, "How about we ask that guy over there who looks bored if he wants to meet us in the family bathroom for a three-way?"

There was no mistaking Josh's look of disdain coupled with his unspoken, "Are you nuts?"

I dribbled a sentence off into the distance, "Well, I just thought it would be kind of …"

I guess I just didn't get it…how to flirt, have fun and be seductive. Obviously, something was wrong with me because it was acceptable for my husband to request that I wear his gift to me - fringy, lace red panties with no matching top. I complied at every request, though at age 34 I wasn't "liberated" enough to try a sexy runway walk from the bathroom to the bed, with sultry eyes and an invitation, "Hey, Big Boy." I just got there and slid under the covers on my side. Okay, so that was probably meeting the minimum requirement from Josh's point of view. I can see that now. But at the time, I thought we were good sexual partners. Of course, what did I know? He left after 20 years of marriage, opting to continue his affair with his legal secretary who was half our age.

So here in this little vignette, the trip to Barbados and my dismissed attempt at flirtatious seduction, was a familiar and embarrassing pattern - great intention and enthusiasm for healthy exploration coupled with zero knowledge of the game of love and how it was played. Granted, I had my dating experience - one boyfriend whom I married, one date rape that was treated as "just part of summer stock theatre," several lame flirtations, and my collection of feedback from family and friends who knew Josh and me.

"They make an awesome couple!" "Meant to be!" "So handsome and classy."

"The buzz is they are doing it like rabbits!!"

And that last comment was from Josh's mom! All of this seemed like positive feedback and a big green light against the backdrop of my own family where Mom and Dad were crazy in love with each other and didn't talk about sex. I never expected them to. In fact, I was glad they didn't. It was their business, and they loved the fun of keeping it to themselves, I guess.

Anyway, I had fumbled around and learned to masturbate in college, keeping *that* to myself. By age 40 I had acquired a vibrator at the recommendation of my psychiatrist who assured me that my partner and I would learn to "enjoy 'turning on' at a slower pace with the help of some additional sex toys." While I wasn't wild about the idea, my second husband, Jack, the sex addict, was totally on board, "The more the merrier!" So I/we learned to accommodate my body which was no longer at "rabbit speed" thanks to ten years on antidepressants.

Monday came. I completed the morning errands which began with driving two hours to Duluth and back, to take William and Molly to school. After a quick stop for groceries, I headed home, put the food away and headed for the bathroom. I thought it would feel good to lie down there because despite its small floor space it had a nearly floor to ceiling window that brought in the glorious morning sun.

I was right, it was small; sunny and small. But I jostled myself around so that I could lie on my back on a towel on the floor with my knees bent. I fit well enough. Lifting my fanny, I pulled my jeans and panties down and applied some lotion. So far so good. I loved the warmth of the sun, being by myself, the quiet of the morning and just breathing. I could forget everything that was scary and just enjoy my own body. I reached for the vibrator which was charged and ready to go at the same time that I heard a knock at our front door.

"*No way,*" I thought to myself. "*Are you kidding me?! Nobody ever comes here. We live in a cabin in the woods for God's sake! It is a rare occasion that I do not know that someone is coming, and gracious hostess that I am, I am at the front door to greet people as they come up the walk; therefore, it is an even rarer occasion that someone knocks!"*

But, sure enough, there was another more persistent knock. I quickly pulled up my pants, stuffed the lotion, vibrator, and towels under the sink, and proceeded to the front door mumbling,

"This cannot be happening, The one time, the *one* time I just want to have an orgasm, somebody comes to visit."

I opened the door and as Claude would say at the start of a scene, "Aaaaaaaaand, we're ACTING!"

"Oh hello," I said with enthusiasm and no sign of distress. The drab looking man with the briefcase standing in a drab overcoat on the front porch of the cabin remained drab.

"Good morning," he replied. "I am looking for Annie Elizabeth McMillan." "That is me," I smiled, "I am Annie Elizabeth McMillan. What may I do for you?"

"I am from the IRS and I have some tax matters to discuss with you. May I come in?" The irony of the situation was beyond words. It reminded me of the oxymoron, "We are from the government, and we are here to help."

I replied. "Of course," stepping aside and motioning him toward the red couch where he sat himself. Leave it to the government, the Internal Revenue Service, no less, to find me at the least opportune time and interrupt at exactly the wrong moment to steal what was to be a perfectly pleasurable few minutes in the midst of the mess of a life I was living. Furthermore, what did I want to bet that this was not going to be good news?

I was right.

The details are now a blur, but the outcome remains crystal clear. I owed taxes and was behind. Did I realize how far behind I was? Additionally, was I sufficiently bullied so that I would do something about it, or would Mr. Drab have to take further action? I assured him I would certainly try to solve the problem, choosing not to mention that I could absolutely guarantee him that my top priority would not change, that being the children. Were they loved, cared for, tummies full and still happy to be on this adventure called life?

Not having established much in the way of rapport, I decided to keep the harsh truth to myself - that I didn't have any money, just day to day survival plans so far. Instead, I looked him in the eyes, dutifully furrowed my brow showing my sincerity in being an upright citizen, and nodded slowly to the words, "I will try."

He left. I went back to the bathroom. I had an orgasm. I hated that he took the edge off my sweet plan, but that orgasm felt great, and I was in control of that part of my life. I got ready to head into Duluth to get William and Molly from school and ballet, stopping only for a moment on the way out the door to write "Back Taxes" on a sticky note for my To Do list.

I had no hope for myself regarding future relationships, meeting someone special, a husband - God forbid. I had racked up two of those who chose to leave, so I really couldn't see the point in trying that again. On the other hand, I did love to be loved and I was the happiest being loving, adding to the joy and delight of someone else's life. I had always been affectionate, loved to touch and be touched, a hugger, and big on back rubs anytime as I was passing behind a chair where my husband's or child's shoulders were inviting someone to squeeze, rub and pat them on the way by. Fortunately, I had William and Molly who easily accepted my love and affection. Many of my needs were met when we three would put in one of our favorite movies, "Planes, Trains, and Automobiles", for example, and snuggle on the big red couch in the cabin.

I fantasized too; especially about a former neighbor of mine upon whom I had a crush. His name was Rod Nichols. He was my age, General Counsel for Control Data Corporation, one of Minnesota's hallmark companies. When we were in our thirties, Rod and his wife, Cammie, General Counsel for Fingerhut, another hugely successful Minnesota company, joined Josh and me for season tickets to the Guthrie Theatre. In addition to that, we would head out to a new restaurant for a culinary adventure every couple of months. Josh and Rod had practiced law together for a short time early in their careers. I knew Rod and Cammie because we attended the same church and because they also lived in the Village of Sunfish Lake. They owned a great home with apple orchards, tennis courts, sailboats, other interesting structures including a guest house and a gazebo overlooking the water. To top it off they cleared a big flat square of green grass where they centered their 13-foot May pole and hosted the Mayfair Celebration for all the village to attend every spring. It was glorious! Just like Rod, who every time he was asked, "How are you?" he would reply, "Splendid!"

Rod and Cammie were always doing something BIG; like making their own apple cider and wine from fruit growing in their yard; tapping their trees in the spring to collect the sap in order to make their own maple syrup; delivering hundreds of plates of cookies to neighbors on the days around Christmas, plates that were brimming with at least a dozen different kinds of cookies, peanut brittle and caramels all homemade in their big old farmhouse kitchen which was a stunner and perfect candidate for Architectural Digest.

Rod was the consummate gentleman with manners and sophistication that wasn't off-putting but simply conveyed his taste for the finer things in life. He reminded me of my dad who was a stickler for manners, firm handshakes and proper etiquette in all situations. Typical vacations for Rod, Cammie and their two daughters were skiing in the Swiss Alps, exploring the canals of Venice, or joining a dig near the Egyptian pyramids. Life appeared to flow with ease as the Nichols family reported on their most extraordinary experiences.

In the fall of 1975 after Josh and I arrived back in the United States from our years in Cambridge, England, we invited Rod and Cammie to join us at North Star Association for a weekend at my parents' cabin. We had a wonderful time. Not only could we dress to the nines to enjoy the theater and fine dining, we could just as easily throw on red and black Lumberjack shirts and jeans to hike the northern Minnesota trails high above Lake Superior. Of course, our duds were from Gokey's, exclusive purveyor of outdoor gear, but we were, nonetheless, four young people, enjoying our early successes in life, active, unpretentious and kind.

One evening at dusk Rod and Cammie took a walk after dinner along Salem Church Road. That was their ritual and neighbors were used to seeing them and exchanging a wave. This night, the Nichols' 18-year-old neighbor looked down at his phone to text something and struck Cathy with the front of his Humvee. She died within hours of arriving at Ramsey Hospital in St. Paul, her two girls barely making it to her bedside to say good-bye. It was a tragedy, a heartbreak, too much to comprehend. The next morning my mom, who was Rod and Cammie's immediate neighbor, and I went to see Rod who had shock in his dark eyes.

"Hello Betty. Hi Annie," he said as he opened the door and accepted our hugs. "Thank you for coming."

The rest of the few minutes that we stayed, were filled with half sentences, aimless looking about or stepping side to side, heads nodding and silence. It seemed enough to just be in the same space. I went to the memorial service which was standing room only at House of Hope. After that I just thought about how much I wanted to step into Rod's life, to match his energy, to care for him, to blend our families. That was not going to happen. I was married, but I thought about it.

Now twenty years later and two marriages with divorces under my belt, I was on the North Shore as fall was in full swing with winter just around the corner. I was out by myself in our front yard splitting wood because we needed logs for the fireplace and because I had learned that the cold temperatures added to the ease of splitting. It is what you did to prepare for winter on the North Shore, so I was told by the caretakers of North Star Association and the folks of Two

Harbors. Therefore, that's what I learned to do. I enjoyed swinging the ax and taking aim at the splitting maul. I loved the fact that I was strong and had a decent aim because these logs answered with a loud crrrraaaack ringing out into the air and into the woods behind me. I picked a spot in the yard where I could see William and Molly in the house in front of the fire, watching a funny movie while I was outside on my own doing an adult thing that gave me a sense of satisfaction. It was a way I could step away from parenting responsibilities without leaving the children. And leave them I did for the log splitting daydream about Rod Nichols.

There I was, in my blue jeans, my Lumberjack shirt, my Gokey's down vest, my heavy socks and work boots, swinging the ax and picking up newly split logs to make a brand-new stack to be burned in our fireplace. The air was cold, I could see my breath each time I exhaled in the still night that was graced with a full moon and trillions of stars. Nowhere, nowhere in the world has as many stars as the pitch-dark nights on the North Shore. It took my breath away then and I know it always will.

Then in the distance, coming down the dark road that became our driveway, was Rod, walking toward me in the male version of matching outdoor gear. He approached in silence and stopped within a few inches of my now quiet posture. He took the ax from my hands and set it down. He looked at the pile of split logs, obviously impressed, but said nothing about that. He simply put his arms around me and pulled me toward his body as he leaned down and kissed me fully on the mouth. It was a long kiss that ended slowly. We both leaned back a little. I was quiet and Rod said, "Annie, I found you. I have been in love with you since the moment we met, when you and Josh and Cammie and I spent time together. I have been healing, coming to terms with what I want for the rest of my life. I knew you were here, and I decided to come and see for myself - if what I hoped to be true really existed. Finding you, outside on this cold night, in the midst of your life, carrying on, is what I hoped for. I have always been drawn to you. I love your spirit, your grit, the adventure and the fun in you, and I am intrigued with all I do not know yet. Will you come with me, be my wife, go on adventures with our children, find causes to serve, and honor God with two lives well-lived?"

And as I blinked back the tears and opened my lips to say, "Yes," the still night exploded with, "Mom! Mom! The oven is on fire! Molly tried to make nachos and the oven is on fire!!"

"Okay. I'm coming!" I yelled. "Molly get outside. William, show me. Grab that towel, we'll smother it and if that doesn't do it, we'll grab the fire extinguisher. Whooooo! That's *hot*! Get me one more big towel from the bathroom. I think we've got it. Okay, no problem. Open the sliding doors and leave the front door open. Molly you can come in again. Everything is out and we are all safe. No harm done."

"Molly, I *told* you to keep the oven door sightly open when you make nachos," shouted William."

Not cowed by William, Molly shot back, "I know! I just forgot!"

"Hey, nice recovery everyone," I piped in…just me, no Rod. "It happens to everybody, so don't worry about it, Molly. Burning food until it catches on fire is part of learning to cook. When the oven is on broil, the oven door stays open a bit.

"You've got that now, right?" Molly's nod in the affirmative was all that was required.

"William, good thinking and great decision to call me for help," I added. "We've got a smoky cabin for the night, and we'll have to bundle up in blankets for the next 15 minutes so we can let the smoke out. But beyond that, we're in good shape. Should we make a new batch of nachos?"

"Ummm, maybe" said Molly with a smile while William looked less than excited about a do-over. We decided not to make the nachos. Besides it was cold in the cabin, we were busy bundling up and the appeal of snacks had passed. My fantasy went up in smoke too, so to speak, but it was available and one I re-played whenever I was out alone in the woods, feeling lonely, missing my husbands, feeling lovable but not the recipient of some adult male's love.

Chapter 14
Where It All Began

The whole pet thing had a life of its own, mostly nutty. I now appreciate it as a brilliant diversion that kept us busy when reality tried to creep in and tempt me to conclude, "We're screwed." I couldn't have *that,* so I was happy to go with the flow, or lack thereof, when it came to our pets. As far as I was concerned, if something, anything, made us happy and brought joy to our new lives, it was worthy of consideration. "I will find a way," was my attitude and I meant it. Underneath my adventurous spirit that I trotted out every day disguised as Molly and William's mom, was also red-hot fire in my belly regarding Jack, ignited by his "I'm not coming" phone call.

There wasn't a day that I didn't spend time just standing in the cabin, the phone receiver that had dangled from the wall, now back in place. My hands would rest comfortably on my hips, as I looked out of the floor-to-ceiling glass windows onto Lake Superior. I breathed deeply as I took Her in. She never ceased to stop me in my tracks and bring me to a moment of wonder. I could tell where Her Majesty met the sky; but except for that, Lake Superior was all I could see. She was mesmerizing - vast, a dark inky blue, shimmering in the sun nearer to shore, and deep. Deep like the biggest breath I could take when I closed my eyes and plunged myself into her freezing cold water, swimming down, and down some more to touch a boulder; but not even coming close, kicking for dear life to find the surface and breathe again. Deep like a guttural roar, strong, powerful and omnipotent. That's what I saw. That's what I felt. That's what I knew to be true and good and mighty.

Her Majesty wrapped Herself around me each day, engulfing all my senses if not from looking at Her, from memories of growing up on the North Shore. The uncontrollable shivers from dips in her freezing cold temperatures when I was all of five years old; my understanding of the raw power of the natural world from her wild nor'easter storms and crashing waves. Sweet, summer nights as a little girl falling asleep in Sve's cabin number six under piles of quilts while she gently caressed the shore; falling in love over and over again with her essence, water, and never tiring of thirst-quenching mouthfuls that put any other drinking water to shame. Finally, her air, her amazing air that rose from the surface of her cold waters, moving across the land giving life to the North Shore. Just by breathing her pure, cool, abundant air, she filled me with the spirit of God and energy that made me feel invincible.

I knew Lake Superior when she dressed in fog, slow waltzing all night long to the foghorn at Split Rock Lighthouse. I knew her when I was four and fell into her shallow waters, cutting my head four stitches worth. I knew her when she wept with me because she understood the hole in me when my father died. I knew her when I actually did have sex on her beach, and when I walked my babies to sleep along her pebbly shore.

And I knew her at the end of the day that Jack called, trusting her as I stood still with an overwhelming sense that I was right where I was supposed to be. She placed me in the palm of God's hands - the God I knew, the God who could create such beauty and magnificence and who surely wouldn't abandon me and the children.

I remembered when early on I stood in the cabin, breathing deeply, hearing myself say, "You fucker. You fucker! I don't give a rat's ass what you do or don't do. All I know is that you are *not* taking me down and, by God, you are *not* going to ruin the lives of William and Molly" (as if I had that kind of power.)

My children are going to have incredible childhoods and amazing lives. Get the *hell* out of my way."

I wasn't loud; I didn't need to be. I was seething, fists clenched, and I was committed. Besides, Her Majesty had my back.

From that moment on, when it came to anything William or Molly wanted: pets of all kinds, musical instruments, clothing, lessons, camps, the latest video games, a car, a trip to Disney World or friends, I always leaned toward yes. That doesn't mean I didn't use my brain or ever say no; I was simply of the mind that anything could be done with some problem solving and a little creativity. A husband and money were promptly relegated to the "nice to have" column, and since they were non-existent in my case, they couldn't be necessary or "must have." In many ways I never looked back. I was determined not to let our circumstances beat our desires out of us.

I had my own history with family pets having grown up with golden retrievers. Reveille was our first family dog, spectacular in her regal demeanor, kind and loving to us all and blessed with fine features and a very pretty face which I guess was why she had so many litters. At least once a year we would watch new puppies suckling on Reveille when they hadn't even opened their eyes, snuggling and crawling over each other on the mismatched towels covering the tile floor of our downstairs bathroom. During birthing, Mom let us watch as long as we sat quietly. As the puppies grew, we were allowed to help more and more, gently moving them so they could get their mama's milk, making sure the runts of the litter weren't left behind.

Reveille lived a good life as our family dog. She passed the baton or bone, I guess you could say, to Shauna, one of her puppies, who took her place and whom I especially loved. Shauna was the best babysitter when Oliver Sundance, my first-born son was one year old and learning to walk. She stayed right by him at just the right distance as Sundance toddled between the gardens, the birch and apple trees on the lawn sloping toward Hornbeam Lake behind my childhood home.

In 1959, when I was in 5th grade, my parents had bought three of the ten, 5-acre lots in Sunfish Lake Village. Paul Williamson, a family friend and land developer around the Twin Cities, spoke with my parents early on about his plans to sell the land. Paul's family owned most of the land south of Highway 110 once you crossed Salem Church Road, property that was hilly, flush with oak, elm and willow trees, little ponds and one lake, Hornbeam. The land was ripe for development in the exclusive village of Sunfish Lake and a gem of a purchase for the families who were in the right place at the right time.

There were two homes already there before Paul opened his land for sale. One belonged to his sister Marnie. She owned a big old white three-story farmhouse surrounded by crooked fences that somehow kept cows, horses, pigs and chickens where they were supposed to be. Add to the animals, salt blocks, rusty troughs of water, several wooden feeders stuffed with hay and of course, mud - lots of mud no matter what the season of the year. Marnie's farm was there first before Sunfish Lake's affluent population arrived. It was more than a little too rustic for everyone's taste and yet it remained an unsolvable eyesore that was simply referred to as "The Williamson Farm," code for "Yeah, we all know what we think about that."

Marnie accessed her farmhouse by turning her banged-up red pickup onto her dusty, dirt driveway off Delaware Ave. Taking the potholes and puddles at a pretty good clip, she would arrive in a cloud of dust at her unpretentious side door which functioned as her main entrance. Marnie was around 50, lived alone, ran the farm herself and was on the gruff side. For as long as I knew her, she had one look, well-filled-out Oshkosh overalls over a worn, large size plaid wool shirt, black rubber Wellington boots, gray hair pulled back in a low bun, no make-up and no smile. Actually, I did see a half smile try to take hold once, when we returned one of her runaway dogs.

The other home belonged to Marta and Ethan Carlson located one dirt road further south of Marnie's driveway and on top of a higher hill. Ethan and Marta were a class act and balanced Marie Williamson in an interesting sort of way. The Carlsons were great outdoors people whose ranch style home beautifully displayed all things L. L. Bean. Deceptively big as it stretched out along the ridge overlooking Hornbeam, the Carlson home was perfectly maintained by Ethan who was always outdoors making headway on his To Do List unless he was taking a break to re-light his pipe or add another homemade bird feeder to the property. Ethan himself blended into his surroundings, padding around in woodsy colors while Marta carried the extroversion component for the two of them, always ready with home-made cookies and time for a good chat on one of their decks whenever we walked over to visit. If no one answered our knock, Ethan and Marta were more than likely at their second home of equal beauty on an island at the Canadian border in the Boundary Waters. They generously shared their cabin in the summer, and their backyard gazebo on winter snow days when all of the neighborhood that surrounded Hornbeam would toboggan or snowshoe over for hotdogs and chili. Carlsons set the standard for being good neighbors which amazingly attracted seven more families of like-minded generosity and fun.

We were the first family to purchase Paul's lots, building our new home on top of a hill surrounded by alfalfa fields that stretched to the lake. Our particular lots were barren, no trees, except for a few old oaks leaning over the water intertwined at ground level with grape vines and buckthorn. All of the lots had acreage in Hornbeam Lake, named for the hornbeam trees Paul planted near the shore. The hornbeam tree looked like a stick drawing by a preschooler, but the spring-fed lake that bore its name was glorious for all of us who came to own a piece of it. Every family contributed docks, rafts, canoes, row boats and our very own sailfishes built to order by one of our new neighbors, Bjorn Cary who took my brother Robby under his wing as his apprentice. Throughout the summer months, I and my two 6th grade girlfriends, who lived on either side of me, floated on air mattresses reading Nancy Drew books when we weren't swimming, sailing or begging our brothers to take us hunting for turtles.

Winter was even better! We shoveled rinks for hockey and broomball and paths as far down the lake as we could before we ran out of shoveling energy. Best of all, the frozen lake was home to the final yards and finish line of our self-designed ice slide, a 50-yard chute built out of packed snow: the McMillan kids' version of the luge. Originating at the top of the hill next to our house, we perfected our design and construction to produce a ride with ever increasing speeds and thrills over the winter, meticulously icing the trough with pails of water hauled from the laundry room, until our frozen mittens called it done.

Even as novices, when I was 12 and my brother Robby was 10, we showed entrepreneurial promise, especially Rob who grew into an inventor, designer, architect, and builder. Our life in the country was free as in freedom. Not much was ever out of bounds. Mom and Dad were enthusiastic about our ideas and encouraged us to get out there and try to make them happen. Dad even promised he would go down our ice slide that first winter when we were finished building it and needed an adult to see if it really worked.

My dad had contracted polio as an eight-year-old boy, but for the longest time I never noticed. Legs were good if you had them, I guess, but if not, they were "nice to have" vs. "must have." No one said that. I never heard that. I just didn't especially think of my dad's legs as necessary for *him* because he just handled it. He walked with leg braces and crutches, and also used a wheelchair to get around. He moved around just fine to my eye. I never thought he looked not okay. He moved energetically and used what was around him - the car door, a chair, an ottoman, or a couch for balance when he was getting up and down, but nothing stopped him from a full and robust life.

My father, Robert McMillan, Jr. was a respected patent lawyer at Oppenheimer Law Firm, married to my mom, Elizabeth, Macalester's 1942 Homecoming Queen. Dad was a former state champion swimmer who practiced in the Mississippi River where the upstream currents provided the challenge he needed. He was a wrestler, a pilot, a committed Christian with a powerful faith, a tireless volunteer for the Society for the Blind, an elder on the Session at House of Hope Presbyterian church, and a role model for those who found themselves with a disability. As a family, we camped, canoed and fished in the Boundary Waters. Dad flew to Canada to fish with my brothers. He whooped us all at ping pong, loved singing opera, and playing the ukelele. Dad was rugged handsome with a magnetic smile and a handshake that pulled you in every time. He was a gentleman with impeccable manners, irreverent as hell, crazy about my mom and game for anything. He was humble, loved his family, and best of all, my dad told great stories. He found a way to do everything, more than any other fathers I knew.

Robby and I weren't the least bit surprised when Dad said he would go down our ice slide on the toboggan, so we met him at our starting line at the top of the hill. Per Dad's request we fetched a redwood picnic table bench for him to use as he negotiated his descent to the snow-covered ground. Dad showed up ready in his red and black lumberjack shirt, khaki pants, fur-lined leather winter gloves and a dark brown fur Russian Cossack hat. In no time Dad had situated himself midway back on the toboggan, sitting up straight and taking a good hold of the ropes on either side. With one final adjustment to his hat and a huge grin he bellowed, "Okay kids. Let 'er rip!"

We scooted the toboggan to the edge of the hill, Dad leaned forward past the tipping point and the toboggan started to gather speed, a lot of speed. Launch successful! Unaware that paralysis from polio eliminates fat, tissue and muscle around the bones, we never gave any thought to Dad's comfort going down the slide. The toboggan once had a thin pad, but we never even used it so it was no longer there. We were all about speed and staying in the trough. That's why we took the luge in saucers, experiencing the ridge and three-foot drop just before the lake as little more than an exciting bump.

In Dad's case, he was airborne.

"JESUS H. CHRIST!" we heard him holler when the toboggan landed and finally stopped way past the finish line. "WHOA that smarts! Get your mother!"

"Dad! Dad! Are you okay?" we shouted, running down the hill as fast as we could.

"We're coming! WOW - you were flying! That was neat!! We're coming! Are you okay? WOW!"

He was okay as far as we knew. He must have been because all he ever talked about was what a great ice slide we built and how to make it better. Not another word about hurt or polio or "I'm never doing that again."

"Put me down for next year and the improved version," was all we heard, "and count your mother in, too."

I also grew up with horses which I rode with my same neighbor girlfriends after school. We had blankets and western saddles, but I often just rode bareback. Brownie, our 20-year-old, swayback gelding which my parents bought from our neighbor across the road, had quite a nice saddle already built in. Brownie was gentle, brown and unimpressive with a look about him as if to say, "I have had an interesting life, but it was many years back now. Don't ask me."

Brownie had been a jumper in his day, which I discovered when I was lying on my back on his back down by the lake. It was a perfect summer day, sunny and warm, and I was happy to be riding by myself. I watched the white cumulus clouds move in and out of the shapes of animals to the sound of the lake lapping at the shore. Squinting as I looked up through the birch trees, I was unaware of the fallen birch branch two feet off the ground in front of Brownie. It proved to be too much of a temptation, I guess, because Brownie suddenly jumped it without my permission or command. I went from close to dozing to close to in the lake. I didn't care. The ground was mossy, and I wasn't hurt, but I sure was surprised and impressed, imagining I had a real champion jumper that probably no one knew about!

I dusted myself off and jumped back on with a new respect and curiosity about "good ol' Brownie." I thought to myself, *"Why, he has been fooling me with this low energy 'I don't want to go' behavior when we first leave the pasture for a ride. He can move, when he wants to. I just experienced it, and yet I exhaust myself kicking and clucking him along just to get him to trot. This feigned reluctance has all been an act!"*

I had to give him credit. He was smarter than I thought and he knew it, figuring I wouldn't catch on. The net result, up until he jumped the log, was that he did whatever he wanted like eat any clover, in any field, any time, any place, often stopping dead in his tracks for a sweet nibble. That gave me whiplash not to mention ruining the rhythm of a relaxing ride. On the other hand, there was a built-in sweet contrast because the best part of every ride began at the moment we turned in the direction of home. Brownie would break into a gallop, not slowing down until he had reached the pasture gate. We'd fly like the wind all the way to oats, hay, and maybe an apple.

Days later, our neighbor did, in fact, confirm Brownie's jumping reputation. For a short while, my newly discovered champion obliged me while I set up a few jumps and found paths with downed trees to spice up our rides. It turned out to be more work than fun, so we agreed to be good sports about our limitations, happy with riding our beautiful paths with an exciting moment every now and again.

I learned how to brush, bathe, and feed all our animals. The dogs were pretty easy; they were more like siblings to me than the horses. I was fascinated with the horses, mysterious and muscular, powerful and strong with big, beautiful eyes. I eagerly watched when their hooves were filed, and their shoes changed. When winter came, I learned how to coax Brownie and Tejas, our two-year old quarter horse, into a horse trailer and how to tie them off. I loved riding along in the truck to their winter home on a Minnesota farm an hour away where they stayed in a warm barn with other animals. I loved being outside walking in my cowboy boots. I loved sitting on hay bales and climbing in the huge barn where my grandfather stored hundreds of bales of hay for the winter. I loved feeding the horses oats, apples, and carrots. I loved learning the whistle that always worked to call them in. I loved my tan riding pants, especially in the fall when they kept me warm while the horses' hooves crunched along on orange, yellow and red leaves that had fallen to the ground. And I especially loved seeing the horses' breath in the air as they snorted through their noses when the temperatures dropped.

I was happy and invigorated in my Annie Oakley days. Animals were a part of my family and I wanted that for my children, too.

Chapter 15
Cocoa - Another Angel

Cocoa joined our family when William was seven and Molly was two. Cocoa was a mutt/mix of Pekingese and Shih tzu on death row in a family that hoarded pets. I met him because I felt him brushing up against the back of my legs while I sat in a cushioned wicker chair under which he hid. We were on a very small porch with five other people, three other dogs and at least 15 cats lounging on various shelves, bookcases, ottomans and arm rests. Our location was an east St. Paul home where I was meeting a family whose son might benefit from Xtarship Friendship, a foundation I had started.

It was a Thursday afternoon in the spring of 1999. I had picked up Christopher, my second-born son from my first marriage, and two of his friends from St. Paul Academy where the boys attended school. They were good-natured 15-year-olds, pals from hockey and willing to offer their friendship to a child their age who was fighting cancer.

The Xtarship Friendship Foundation brought kids together, adding $100 and the use of a laptop to the mix so that new friends could go online to shop for something to do together at the hospital. Pokémon cards, actually anything Pokémon, were popular. Within a week, the kids would be meeting for a second time at the hospital with something to do that took the sting out of what the children had repeatedly said was the worst part of being sick: being alone with no friends their own age.

On this particular Thursday, Christopher and his friends were ready to offer friendship to a 15-year-old boy who lived at Cocoa's residence. After we arrived and got through some chit chat about all the animals, a wet spring so far and the idea of Xtarship Friendship, I made several attempts to interest the Mr.

and Mrs. in a friendship opportunity for their son. I was fielding a lot of silence and one response that peaked in enthusiasm with, "Hmmm, well I s'pose."

I decided to wind it up, suggesting we all think about it, and that the offer was always there for them should they want to start a friendship.

Not able to stop myself as we were making our way toward the screen door of the porch, I asked "What did you say about the dog under my chair and the dog pound?"

"Oh we're taking him back," said Mr. "We've got too many animals. We don't want him. Nobody does, so he's not going anywhere," he added as he raised his eyebrows, making the "cut off his head" motion with his right pointer finger, slicing an imaginary cut across his neck in the air in front of him. And, as if that wasn't clear enough, he added, "If you know what I mean."

"Yes, I think I do." I responded. Then before time or space could pass I added, "I'll take him."

"Suit yourself. Don't know much about him except his name. Cocoa." And that was the last of any conversation before the litany of "Thank you and nice to meet you," from Christopher and his friends.

"Thank you for your time. And the dog," I added.

"All the best to your son. We'd be glad to get to know him."

And then lots of fast walking and bumbling as we hurried down the longer than I remembered sidewalk to the car, jockeying for position as we all got in, trying to identify what we had in our arms and laps - a dog we guessed under a long, dirty, smelly coat of hair that hung longer than his paws, off his tail and covered his whole face save a small black spot that had to be a nose. He was a low riding gray mop.

Mom! What just happened in there? Are we really taking this dog home?" Christopher asked.

"You just got a dog, Christopher," the boys shouted like they couldn't believe what their eyes had just seen.

"Yes. Well, I am taking him home. Christopher lives with his dad, and Cocoa will come with me. We couldn't just leave him there to walk the plank!" I added. "You guys got that didn't you? Those people were going to take him back to the dog pound tomorrow and that was going to be the end of his life!"

"If you know what I mean," I added under my breath.

The back seat proved to be a little too cozy with Cocoa on board, and it wasn't long before the boys were jostling about.

"Phew! P.U. He stinks! You hold him." they called out, elbowing each other for a different seating plan.

I agreed. Cocoa was pungent. But I was driving and a little shaken myself, also wondering what *did* just happen in there, so I left them to figure it out which they did, laughing and taking advantage of the opportunity to bring up poop and farts. All in all the boys were great, fussing over Cocoa telling him it was going to be alright.

Suddenly realizing it was after 5:00 and a school night, I snapped out of it.

"Who's hungry?" I asked.

"I am."

"Me too."

"Me too and Cocoa is. Can we get Burger King?" I heard from the back seat.

"Of course," I replied. Then I turned around to look them in the eyes and added, "Thank you. Thank each of you, boys, for coming along today and offering to be friends. And thank you *especially* for welcoming Cocoa. I guess he is the one who needed your friendship today. For now, let's get some dinner and I'll run you home."

First thing the next morning I booked a Tuesday appointment with a groomer at a posh-looking place I remembered driving by on Grand Avenue in St. Paul. I was a little worried about trying to bathe Cocoa before his appointment, not sure what I would find, so I opted for three simple days that included lots of petting and twenty-minute walks on a leash to the end of the cul-de-sac and back. William and Molly thought having a dog was great. They hugged him, coaxed him along on our walks but mostly sat on the floor with him asking a lot of questions about where were his eyes and ears, and did he have a whole face. When we walked around the puddles at the end of our driveway, Cocoa dragged through them adding a dark dust ruffle to his mop coat. Despite his fragrance which intensified when he got wet, we loved him from the start. I knew he belonged with us.

When Cocoa and I officially met eyeball to eyeball after his appointment on Tuesday, his makeover revealed a most lovable little dog. He looked a bit sheepish with the blue ribbon perched on top of his head. He met my gaze as if to say,

"The groomer did this; it's not me. I usually need a day or two after a trim to get my look the way I like it."

I understood, having had short curly hair all my life, so I had no problem looking past the satin bowed pigtail to see a fine-looking gentleman with a salt and pepper gray coat and a unique, slightly off-center smile which appeared to be a combination of an underbite and characteristic of his Pekingese/shih tzu mix. I always thought it gave him an all - knowing look amidst the drama of our family.

Cocoa became William's dog. They were drawn to each other which turned out to be another blessing. Sensing a big change when we started our new life at the cabin, Cocoa stepped up, staying right by William's side, keeping an eye on his master, a traumatized eight-year-old who was shattered on the inside, and who, by September, couldn't and wouldn't go to school one third of the days of the 3rd grade fall semester.

In June, July, and August before school started, William had coped - on the outside - with summer activities and in my estimation, through the close proximity he had to me and Molly every day. I understood the numbness I saw in William because we were all feeling the shock of Jack's leaving. Thanks to our therapists who labeled the stages of grief, and specifically helped me understand what William was going through, we were able to keep our wits about us and let the process run its course.

William was at the worst age to lose a parent, I learned. Molly was young enough to transition without immediate deep feelings of loss. Those would come later. But William understood his dad was gone *and* that he didn't have a good answer to the question, why. William blamed himself no matter what anyone else said, confused because he had been his dad's best buddy. In addition to reading and hanging out, they took mechanical things apart, biked and skied, and practiced karate. Jack used to joke when he was speaking to parents at karate tournaments about William's accomplishments as a seven-year-old.

"I teach Karate all day from 7:30 to 5:30, driving all over the Twin Cities where I bring classes to my students at their different schools. The *last* thing I want to do when I get home is more karate. But, William meets me at the door in his karate uniform ready to practice so he can test and move onto the next belt level. That, ladies and gentlemen, is how we have a seven-year-old brown belt, an advanced level for any student. William wanted it, he initiated it, he earned it. There were no freebies, in fact, I probably insisted on a little more from him."

I loved seeing the two of them together. William was affectionate and so was Jack, so they cuddled when they read and played video games. We had a happy balance in our family where I often tended to Molly, our youngest and my only daughter, and Jack and William did their guy thing.

When school started, William sank into a deeper depression. On school day mornings, he would simply call from the loft, still in his pajamas, "Mom, I can't go to school today. I don't want to. I can't."

I would climb up three steps of the ladder so I could peer into the futons and blankets knowing William was in there. When I found his face, my heart broke looking into his empty blue-grey eyes, knowing he was lost. I didn't know what he needed, and I don't think he knew what to ask of me. So, we took each day in stride with lots of assurances that this was tough, and that he was making a good choice for himself for that day. I promised him that he would be alright, that he would feel like going to school soon enough and in the meantime, we would see what the day could bring at home.

With the support of his teachers and his therapist, I continued to honor William wherever he was, encouraging him gently to give school a try, but backing off if he didn't respond. Fortunately, William was plenty bright. I knew he would be able to close the learning gap whenever he was ready. I kept a normal schedule in place, taking Molly into school and collecting homework for William which he did without hesitation. We did things together on his days at home, outdoor hikes, cooking, therapy appointments, bathing Cocoa, tending to our property, basically, spending time together which was exactly what we both needed.

The truth was that I didn't know William, and William didn't know me. I loved him with all my heart and was so grateful I had birthed a perfect human being after nine months of self-doubt. It hadn't been easy. My mother and stepdad responded with laughter when I told them I was pregnant.

"You? At your age? How old are you? 45? And you're not married. Well, good luck." That was the extent of their "support" until the day William was born.

On that morning my mom and Beryl arrived at the hospital full of excitement, eager to hold William, congratulate Jack and hug me. Mom left a beautiful note for me and our new baby. Forgiveness happened, easily and sweetly, and I moved on.

Up until William's birth, I was pretty shaky, despite preferential treatment and attention because I qualified as a high-risk mother (age, history of addiction, history of depression, therapy and antidepressants). I struggled to feel okay about myself - and to top it off, I had this recurring dream that William was going to be born without a chin.

"Can you see a chin?" I asked the technician every time I went for an ultrasound, not caring what she thought about my question.

"Your baby's head and profile look perfectly normal," she always told me, "So I think we can all expect to see a chin."

I still asked, right up until the day he was born. That dream was so vivid. Looking back on William's journey through the first six months without his dad, I came to understand what was going on between the two of us. William and I, as the two stronger legs of our three-legged stool of a family, only had each other and we didn't have much of a relationship, at least the kind we were going to need for the road ahead. I could read Harry Potter but so could William. I skied, didn't do karate, liked to figure out how things were put together so I could fix them, but I wasn't a replacement, by any stretch of the imagination, for Jack.

I did, however, stay put. I didn't leave. I showed up every day and told the children whenever I could work it into the conversation that I was there for the long haul. I think William needed to verify that with his own eyes, to check often that I was where I said I would be, to rack up his own data that I was not going to leave. My predictability helped him gain confidence to go on with his life, which was the goal. Little by little we started to get to know each other a day at a time using building blocks that were new and that were our own.

We cooked and by that I mean I cooked while William watched the cooking channel until he saw something he wanted to try. Then he would shop for ingredients, create something wonderful and I would clean up. We played in the water along Lake Superior who was working Her own kind of healing every day. We planned William's ninth birthday party to include a hike up the North Star River to the Upper Falls where he and his friends swam in the natural pool showered by rushing water coming from thirty feet above - Indiana Jones style. We found each other in music and movies, both playing the piano and always good for a marathon of comedy flicks with popcorn. "Planes, Trains and Automobiles," "The Birdcage" and anything Eddie Murphy were always a winning combination. Eventually we cuddled, finding out that we *did* fit together, our mom and son bodies relaxed in an unspoken understanding of trust and safety.

Meanwhile, Cocoa understood that William's well-being depended on being within reach at all times for petting and snuggling. Cocoa sat with William as though he were Player Two from that first summer through years of video games. No one was more attentive than Cocoa during the months that William perfected his Dance Dance Revolution skills. Both gentlemen built nests when they went to bed. Cocoa put far less effort into his, as he had two readymade spots into which he could curl as soon as William lay down - in William's arms against his chest or behind William's bent legs. William, on the other hand, landed on his bed and proceeded to scurry in a circle pulling his blankets with him until he was in the middle of a toasty nest, able to pull as much or as little blanket across himself and Cocoa as the cool of the night required. Cocoa was a great, low maintenance pal, happily accompanying William when we would head out on day trips up and down the North Shore of Lake Superior or leading the way when we would cross country ski out our front door to get to the trails at North Star Association.

Cocoa was by no means a bargain. From the beginning he required catch-up care and feeding which was clearly a new experience for him. He loved the attention.

None of it was burdensome, just extensive and expensive. I loved pampering him because he was oh so agreeable; always eager to have me scoop him up for the next appointment; sitting on the front seat of the car and then curling up quietly on the floor as we made the rounds.

Groomers and veterinarians were always encouraging despite the obvious. We had a project on our hands, but they were tactful in their commentary, avoiding what we both were thinking, "Good God! What happened here?!"

"Oh he'll come back," they'd say confidently. "He's just a little gun shy. All he needs is lots of TLC and don't worry if he backs away. I expect he's been hit a time or two. He's got the makings of a handsome coat…once we get the shine back into it. Nothing that a good diet and grooming won't cure."

Cocoa also required an Invisible Fence, no small investment, to protect him from our ridiculous neighbors who had nothing better to do than complain if our sweet dog accompanied them on their cross-country ski treks. Cocoa got the hang of his new restraint quickly and learned to stay within our property which was expansive with a big deck and crawl space under which he could find safety if some coyote or eagle came visiting.

In 2003 at one of our regular check-ups, our vet sat me down for a chat about Cocoa's mouth which had become very infected. I had no idea. I felt like a terrible mother at the same time I was learning that Cocoa was a candidate for major tooth and gum surgery costing $1800. That was a number not in my budget or vocabulary as we were regulars at the food shelf, and I was trading cleaning for private school tuition.

And why didn't I opt for public school right there in Two Harbors? I was asked that all the time, often with an edge to the question as if I didn't have the right to choose a private education or perhaps more to the point, I didn't have the status because I cleaned houses to even consider a private education. I stopped getting mad at the question when I realized it wasn't about me. If anyone genuinely wanted to know, I was happy to explain that I wanted the best education I could find for my children. I was looking for a community of professional educators to help me raise William and Molly. I wanted a small ratio of teachers to students, a veteran group of teachers who showed up because they loved their jobs and whose values and mine were in alignment, teachers who valued discipline, order, love of country, love of God, kindness and respect for all of creation. I wanted measurement and creativity that ensured accomplishment. I wanted homework, an emphasis on reading and learning to educate oneself. I wanted a teacher who would pick up the phone if they thought I should know about a rough spot in my child's day. And I wanted intervention when children needed to learn to compromise, to listen, to value differences, to ask themselves, "What would Jesus do?"

I found my interests to be grossly underrepresented in public education, and rather than try to change something that was way beyond my control, I chose private education with its requirement for tuition. Paying for it was a problem within my control and worth solving. Furthermore, our fair town of Two Harbors was smack dab in the middle of the meth epidemic in northern Minnesota and I wanted to minimize all exposure to drugs and alcohol. Finally, I made my decisions year-by-year based on what my children needed and who their teachers were going to be. Changing schools never prevented me from moving forward to the next best teacher. The newness and the opportunity to learn from someone who *really* knew what they were doing became part of the adventure. The teachers always came through, and William and Molly thrived.

As I sat quietly without any questions. Our vet, who interestingly was a fellow parent of children at the same private school, helped me out.

"I am afraid it is only going to get worse. There aren't a lot of options if you want to keep him… alive… that is."

That did it. I had learned by then, that sometimes reality, in its most brutal presentation, simply had to be irrelevant when it came to my family. I could always figure out solutions to seemingly insurmountable problems if I was making the right decision.

"Do you have a payment plan, and when can you get him in?" I asked.

"Yes, and you can leave him with us tonight, if you'd like."

The rest was for another day. It took me three years to pay that off. But so what? I was grateful to find myself in the care of a compassionate doctor who accepted my $50 payments for 36 months and never said a word. Cocoa was a much happier dog after the surgery and gratefully, it didn't wreck his smile. Even if I totaled all ten years of Cocoa expenses, that dog was worth every penny and more. He came bearing enormous gifts just like Jesus taught when he said, "I will use the least of these, my brethren."

Cocoa never lost his understated presence. He would pad pad pad pad across the floor in little steps, pretty much under the radar, seemingly going about the business of being a dog. And yet he assumed two of the most important and critical roles in our family. First, he was our protector, obviously not for his size and fierceness, but because he took it upon himself to organize the forest's inhabitants in such a way that our family was safe; ensuring that we all lived peacefully and very happily as all God's creatures.

I don't know how he did it; I just know I looked forward to Cocoa's nighttime ritual of TAPS. As the sun was setting, Cocoa would bark for a good minute to all the critters large and small in the woods around our cabin. As he barked, I'd sing to myself,

> "Day is done. Gone the sun.
> From the lakes, from the trees, from the skies.
> All is well. Safely rest.
> God is nigh."

Then, after one last run to all corners of our property, Cocoa took his place on the corner of the deck while the sun disappeared, and the night settled in. Facing east, looking out and over Lake Superior with the North Star Island way down below, he sat on his haunches and raised his voice to the moon and stars if they were out, or to the darkest of nights when clouds covered the sky. And then Cocoa would bring it home.

"Alright now, listen up!" he barked. "Time to go to bed. Most of you know this, but for you who are new to our little piece of heaven, don't even consider coming close to the cabin, to trample our ferns or eat our garden flowers or dig holes by the front porch. We respect you. We love each and every one of you. All is well now. It has been a good day, and we'll see you all in the morning."

And that, I am convinced, is the reason we were one of two cabin-owning families of the North Star Association with beautiful gardens; and therefore, did not feel it necessary to spend part of every conversation complaining about the animals who were ruining their property.

Second, and most important, Cocoa loved a boy who needed an immense amount of cuddling, touch and adoration. Cocoa was a healer. Cocoa and I had an understanding that he was my dog, too, but only because I fed him and made sure he had everything he required to suit up for the awesome responsibilities he fulfilled.

Chapter 16

Angus

By the time our third summer rolled around, William and Molly were 12 and 7 respectively, and were savvy about making plans for their months out of school. There were only two "survivors" from activities of summers past. One was Heritage Days, during which Molly and I took our place along the main street in Two Harbors to cheer during the parade. We were there for William who played French horn in the marching band; and that was it. No contests, pie eating or otherwise. And two was The Lodge Talent Show, as attendees only.

I was working full time in Duluth as Director of Sales and Marketing at the classically beautiful and historically rich Greysolon Hotel which was re-opening its Ballroom for elegant weddings and parties. I needed to find a babysitter for the summer who could drive, and stay for the day to play, make lunch, and shuttle William and Molly to a variety of activities. I liked Grant who was an after-school helper at St. Mark's. He was a junior at East High school, a good-looking kid with a great smile, and a favorite of Molly's because he would play anything and draw, too. I could see what Molly meant. I immediately liked Grant and I liked the idea of having a boy in the mix for William so I called Grant's parents to ask if I might offer him a summer job. We all met and discussed it and agreed to go forward. I was happy to have Grant lined up.

I had one other new plan in place as a result of a generous offer from our neighbor just a cabin down the road. Angus had written in May to say that he wanted to offer friendship and some time together with William if we were interested. Angus suggested hiking, building some summer projects with tools and just hanging out. I appreciated the offer, ran it by William and agreed to talk about it more when Angus and his wife, Chauncy, arrived in June.

We all knew each other. Chauncy had hired me a couple of years before, to clean and open their cabin for them. Each year they made the drive from Houston, Texas to spend the summer at North Star Association. They had three children, all grown and married except for their youngest son, Jeremiah who had Down syndrome and had recently passed away at the age of 21. Chauncy was an interior designer, very particular about the way she wanted me to clean and care for her cabin. I was a neatnik, happy to have her specificity regarding her wishes, so we hit it off. Angus was a retired Episcopal priest, kind of silly and known for a few songs with actions that he sang every summer around campfires on the beach to the delight and cheers of the North Star Association families.

Seventh grade had just ended for William and in one short year he was excelling at the French horn. Coincidentally, Angus decided to take clarinet lessons which prompted discussions about joining the Two Harbors City Band. William was sort of game. He really liked music and he enjoyed playing French horn at school, so he agreed to give it a try. That meant a weekly commitment to band practice on Tuesday evenings from 7 to 9 and the weekly Concert in the Park on Thursdays at 7:30 pm. Angus picked William up a half an hour before each session while Molly and I did our own thing Tuesday night and then attended every Thursday concert.

There were some issues. The band members were still wearing the original band uniforms from the 1920's. William looked ridiculous in the red wide-legged pants with blue piping down the outside seam and the white poly short-sleeved shirt (not from the 1920's) that was way too big. The red tie and the double-breasted red jacket with gold braided epaulets didn't help. At least William could button everything which was more than some band members could say. The good news is that the uniforms were cleaned, mended, and stored at the school where everyone changed clothes for the Thursday night gigs.

Angus and William always rode together despite my offer to have William hop in with Molly and me after the concerts. Angus was quick to say that the guys always went to DQ to reward themselves for playing a great concert while Molly and I generally went straight home for a different treat and to give the guys some room.

The visual of Angus and William struck me as dorky sweet. Angus was thin, the quirky professor, with balding hair strands near his forehead, age freckles on his arms and hands, glasses, and a walk like a duck, side-to-side with his head up as if he was waiting for inspiration. It suited him to be carrying a long, thin instrument case for his clarinet.

In contrast, William was wide, barrel-chested with broad shoulders, lots of short wavy brown hair, unblemished skin save a few summer freckles across his nose, and a walk that leaned forward into the future. Handling the case for his French horn was no problem, in fact, like all stuff in relation to William, it was an extension of him. Whatever he embraced out of curiosity, he swallowed up. His brain was always onto the next thing because the present just didn't seem to be complex enough to keep him totally occupied. I wondered what in the world William and Angus ever had to talk about - unless Angus had another life as a chemical engineer.

Around about the beginning of August, William told me he didn't want to do anything with Angus anymore. It was a Monday, at the end of a workday when I had just gotten home. Grant was no longer our summer sitter having organized an outing where he sat William and Molly on the banks of the Lester River while he jumped off the railroad trestle 55 feet above the water. That, plus his morning agenda which included a two-hour nap while William and Molly made their own breakfasts, did it.

We carried on for the rest of the summer with no replacement for Grant. It worked reasonably well, mainly because my sister, Claire, was at North Star Association for several weeks of vacation and planned something every day that included the children.

Claire's son, Matt was William's age and her daughter, Lizette, 17, was Molly's absolute favorite cousin. The girls had make-up, dress-up and baking chocolate chip cookies in common, while Claire could literally immerse William and Matt in Gooseberry Falls for hours or in front of Mario Bros video games.

I was so grateful for Claire's help, because we only had Angus on the calendar for band and anything else he and William planned together.

"Why don't you want to do anything with Angus?" I asked, setting everything from the workday down on the table where I sat across from William. I was concerned.

"Because today when I woke up Angus was sitting right by my bed looking at me." I was sick.

"That's not okay. What happened?" I asked.

"I told him I didn't want to do anything today, and I went to get Molly."

"What did Angus do?"

"He left. There's more, Mom. I don't like him. He takes me up to the bench (a scenic spot just behind our cabin where a split rail wooden bench looked out over Lake Superior) and says stuff like this is between just us - guy talk - that it can be confusing growing up with lots of feelings that are hard to understand,

and he will help me with those. Plus, when he drives to band and the DQ, he leans over and puts his hand on my leg. I don't like him."

"Got it," I said, "Angus is *over*, William. You don't ever have to go near him again. I'll handle it. I'm so glad you told me. That is so wrong, and you are absolutely right in not liking any of what Angus has done. Thank you so much for telling me. Is there anything else? I am so sorry."

I was furious but took William's hand across the dining room table where we were sitting and firmly repeated, "I've got this. You are safe and Angus is history." Then I walked around the table to give William a hug and asked,

"Can you and Molly hang in there a couple of minutes before I start dinner?"

Whatever their response, I was grabbing the phone to call my therapist, Thea. It was after hours but I laid it out for her other answering machine. Angus was grooming William, and I wanted to confront Angus. Could she help me and what all did I need to do for the children?

The next morning Thea called and opened up her schedule for a 4:00 pm appointment later that day. I called my boss and stayed home from work, deliberately parking my car outside in the driveway for Angus to see should he consider coming our way. We left the cabin at 3:00 to meet Thea. Needless to say, we were skipping band practice. I hadn't said a lot to William and Molly except that I was staying home for the day and that we had an appointment with Thea before dinner at our favorite Chinese restaurant.

Molly was included even though I was concerned about her age and what we would be talking about. But she sure as hell wasn't leaving my sight. Neither of them were until I re-grouped. Armed with paper, crayons and favorite books, we arrived on time and sat down with Thea in her office. William wasn't wild about being there, but I told him we needed some coaching so that I could be sure I was completely prepared to handle Angus and so that we could all learn how to stay safe.

Thea was unbelievably skilled and helpful. We couldn't have been in better hands. She was smiling when we walked in, greeting us with how glad she was to see us all. She summarized what I had told her without dwelling on details but clearing with William that she understood the gist of his concerns.
William said little but nodded to indicate he agreed that she understood.

"Okay good," she said and then went on, "Molly, I am going to spend a few minutes talking to Mom and William. Are you happy with coloring at this table while I do that? If we need you, I'll let you know." And she arranged a spot for Molly facing away from the three of us as soon as Molly said, "Okay."

"William," she began, "you have done exactly the right thing, telling your mom that you are uncomfortable, that you do not like what has been going on with Angus. You are completely right. It is very uncomfortable to have someone looking at you when you wake up. It is inappropriate for him to touch you or say things that are supposed to be a secret. Your instincts are right and speaking up was the exact right thing to do."

William was silent, listening, and nodding a little.

Thea was formidable in her physical presence and in the way she spoke. She was 5' tall, 3' wide, 50 years old with blond, gray hair and a little raspy edge to her voice which always came off to me like she had been out barking orders at someone and was not to be messed with. When she sat down in her chair, a recliner that she flipped into ottoman position with a quick pull on the handle on the side of the chair, court was in session, and it was down to business.

"William, you have done your part, and the rest is up to your mom. So, I am going to talk now about what she will say and how you will work together. We'll even practice before you leave."

"I don't want to be there," said William. "You have to be there," said Thea.

"Well, I don't want to say anything," said William "You won't have to. I promise." Thea replied.

"Now to you, Annie. Ask Angus to come over; the sooner the better, no later than the day after tomorrow. Find a safe place for Molly to be busy in another room. Be at the door when Angus approaches. Do not wait for him to knock. Open the door, and ask him to come in. William will be sitting at the table, eyes on you." She continued, "Do not ask Angus to sit down. Remain standing and look him straight in the eye. Begin. Thank him for coming over. Tell him you know what he is doing. You know he is a predator and that you are onto him. Tell him you know that he has walked into your home uninvited, that he has talked with William about inappropriate subjects and that he has crossed personal boundaries with William. Tell him it is over, that he is no longer to have any contact with you or the children, that he is never to set foot on your property again. Have you got it?"

"Yes," I answered.

"He will try and pull William in by looking past you and going right to William with feigned surprise." Thea started in again. "He'll say something in a lighthearted way like, 'Oh wait a minute. Slow down, there must be some misunderstanding. We were just enjoying time together, right Will? We've had some good laughs and just some good guy times together,' at which point you do not respond, William. And Annie, you cut Angus off. William, keep your eyes on your mom. Do not look at Angus. Do not let him pull you in. Eyes on Mom and she will handle Angus."

Thea wound it up with, "Annie, when I say cut him off, I mean it. Get loud. Say 'No!' or 'Stop Angus!' or 'Angus, I am on to you. You are through.' Then finish with 'Get out and don't ever come back.' Questions? Do you think you can do it? William? Annie?"

When William and I said we thought so, Thea said, "Let's try it."

We role played and earned ourselves a high five. William looked sick while I was ready for bear. Next steps for us were going through the motions of something we usually loved dinner at the China Cafe. We had our usual, one family-size order of pork fried rice and three waters. It seemed so pathetic, but it filled us up and our spirits were lifted, a bit.

As soon as we got home, I called Angus and left a message on his answering machine asking him to please come over at 5:00 the next day. I hardly slept that night. I rehearsed my part several times during the day until I knew my lines. Finally, 5:00 pm arrived. I opened the door as Angus stepped onto our porch.

"Hello Angus. Thanks for coming over. Please come in," I began as I motioned and moved him in toward the table where William was sitting.

"Oh, hi William," Angus said to the boy statue whose hands were folded on his lap and whose eyes were laser-focused on me.

That was the last thing Angus said, except for trying to engage William. I took a breath. Angus's beady, little, black pupils behind his wire rim glasses were particularly creepy which helped as I laid into him. He played his part just as Thea had predicted. We were ready for him. I cut him off. I said everything I wanted to say while William didn't move, right up to and through the sendoff. I was on fire. I never looked away from Angus, staring him straight in the eyes which effectively moved him to sideways shuffle toward the door as I was winding up.

"You messed with the wrong mama, Angus. Don't you ever, *ever* set feet on my property again, you son of a bitch. Now get out." I growled as I closed the door behind him.

"Are you okay, William?" I asked. "You did a great job. You can come out now, Molly," I added as I huffed around the cabin with clenched fists, making some guttural sounds and shaking as I took a lot of deep breaths, a better choice than ripping something to shreds or doing physical damage to our beloved cabin. William eventually moved, and we called it, "Well done and over."

I would like to say that was the end of Angus, but it wasn't. He remained arrogant. I think he thought he could scare me. I could feel the invitation to fight. I sensed he now wanted to take me down more than he wanted to pursue William.

"Game on. Bring it!" I thought. And he did for the rest of summer and the start of the school year. When the children and I left for St. Peter's School in Duluth at 6:45 in the morning, Angus would be standing at the top of our hill right on the property line, with his dog in his arms, the same breed as Molly's puppy, Princess. He stood there, stroking his little dog, and never moved other than nodding one nod as we drove by.

Two years later, this morning ritual with Angus made sense in the worst possible way. As far as I know he left William alone at band practice and the concerts. I drove William to all things band, of course, and I watched him like a hawk. The word according to Chauncy and therefore, around North Star was that "Annie and Angus had some kind of falling out."

Chapter 17

Pet Story - The Next Generation

Being a single mother and vulnerable to guilt from who knows where, makes for crazy head space. Without you even knowing it, guilt slithers into your thinking, so that you actually believe on some level you are not doing enough or are somehow depriving your children because you don't have a husband. I can see it now, but I couldn't identify how crazy I was when I made a lot of pet decisions early on.

For example, if it fell into the category of pet, I bought two, one for each child. In our first pet experience we brought home two bunnies from the summer 4-H fair in Two Harbors. They were both white and black with different markings so we could tell them apart, and I thought, a fine addition to our life which was rapidly falling apart. Of course, we purchased a cage, food and wood chips, so as far as I was concerned we were set with our feeding and cuddling plan. William named his bunny Zeus, and Molly named hers Ziggy. Within one week, Ziggy got out of his cage, got stuck in the outdoor woodpile and died. Zeus carried on, as did we all using the opportunity to talk about "accidents happen."

Shortly thereafter we took a trip to PETCO. We walked in looking for dog food and walked out with dog food, two hamsters and a honking big cage so that our "new friends" could play. Louie, William's hamster, and Zeus, Molly's hamster seemed to be off to a good start, so I thought. Within two days, Louie had eaten Zeus. It was heartbreak for Molly but somewhat lessened by the shock of it all.

"Mom! Molly! We have a problem in the hamster cage. Get up here quick!" William called from the loft. Scurrying up the ladder as fast as we could, we joined William in a chorus of "EEEeuuu's," before the tears. Molly was devastated. Even naming her hamster Zeus, the same name William had used for his bunny, didn't prove to be enough insurance against the pet winds of fate.

I called PETCO the next day, only to I learn that we should not have picked out two male hamsters.

"We generally advise against that because two males will try to kill each other if they are in the same cage," Mr. Rodent manager explained.

"Well, we generally weren't advised of that when we bought two males from you two days ago," I replied. I asked if they would provide another hamster.

When Mr. Rodent Manager agreed to do just that, I attempted another version of "accidents happen" for Molly who was more than a little sensitive after losing two pets. Still, she decided to try again. This time Molly took a different tact, and we brought home a female white rat she named Uncle Buck.

Within a week, a sharpened number two pencil positioned, point first, toward the cage, stabbed Uncle Buck to death because a stuffed animal fell at just the right/wrong angle causing the pencil to plunge into Uncle Buck who was sleeping, presumably, in the wrong spot at the wrong time.

Once again, we were talking about accidents, but this time having to answer the first question out of Molly's mouth, "Why do my animals always die?" "It seems like that," I started when William corrected me,

"Well, actually, Molly, it *is* like that but that doesn't mean anything - like you did something wrong or that you should think that will always happen. It just happened this time… and the other two times."

"I don't want another pet," said Molly. End of conversation.

Thank God for Cocoa, our north star through it all, our go-to pet when things weren't going well. The only downside was that Cocoa hung out with William for the most part, and Molly knew it.

"Do you want a dog? Your own dog?" I asked Molly, when she commented sometime later that William had a bunny, a hamster *and* a dog.

"Yes," she answered, so the next weekend we took a trip to the North Shore animal shelter to see if there was a dog available that might like to "sit on the couch next to me when I knit," Molly explained on the car ride to town. "That's why I want my own dog."

I got that. I understood. Besides evening the score on the number of pets per child, Molly wanted her own companion who would like to do what she wanted. Well, wouldn't you know it, when we walked down the second row of cages at the shelter, we met Snickers who was looking for a home. Snickers was older, a cute little mutt with white, brown and gray markings, a terrier or some such little dog with a great name. Molly and I decided she was perfect so we asked her if she would like to be Molly's dog. As I drove us home, mission accomplished, I just hoped to God that Snickers would last a week.

Molly was in second grade and had learned to knit from her grandma. Molly was amazingly good at her new skill and tried like crazy to have Snickers just sit, sit! SIT! on the couch next to her. Snickers never really got it, but she did stay alive and exhibited other redeemable qualities that created an unbreakable bond with Molly. For three years, Snickers shared a relaxed pace of life with Cocoa by day, and peaceful nights sleeping next to Molly, their two heads on the same pillow. The only drawback, and it wasn't a small one, was that Snickers would pee whenever anyone came near her. She was always excited and friendly, so cleaning up after her just became part of life with Snickers. Somehow, it seemed to me a small price to pay after what Molly had been through.

When Molly and William got ready to visit her dad for a weekend, we had to leave the cabin, not knowing Snickers' whereabouts. She had been gone for five days. Nothing in our searches of Two Harbors, talking with our neighbors up and down the Shore and inquiring at animal shelters from Duluth to Silver Bay, produced any clues. Molly was sad and scared. We all were. It was hard to know what else to do but to carry on and trust that somehow Snickers would be back.

When I got home from the round trip to Hinckley, the well-known halfway point for divorced families when one parent lived on the North Shore and one lived in the Twin Cities, I walked out onto our deck in the cool North Shore air, aching for Molly and calling Snickers' name for the thousandth time. Hoping that by some miracle she would come running, I heard nothing. The forest was still as was Lake Superior. As I turned to walk back into the cabin's soft lights and warmth, I noticed the unmistakable smell of something rotting. My heart sank, nothing moved and the night got even more quiet. I knew something dead was nearby.

Stepping off the deck and kneeling down on the grass, I peered into the dark under the deck. I really hoped I wouldn't see anything, though I already knew I most likely would. My eyes didn't take long to adjust to the dark, and I didn't wonder what I saw. There was Snickers, under the deck, out of my reach, curled up, her collar visible, and not moving.

I called Ted, our good friend and the assistant foreman at North Star. I asked him if he could help me. The next day he came and pulled Snickers out from under the deck, her body already decomposed beneath her sweet coat of many colors.

"I've got her collar for you," he told me over the phone. "She was - well, there was not much left of her, but I dug a grave on the hill by the deck and set her in it as best I could. You'll see the mound." I couldn't speak.

"You know, there was no sign of an attack by another animal. She might have just died of old age," Ted carried on. His voice was soothing, and I was able to hear what he said. "Dogs know when it's their time and they come home to a place where they know they are safe. They just go to sleep. That's what they do. She died where she wanted to be, near you and in her own place."

"Okay," I said through my tears. "Thank you so much Ted. Molly is gone but I'll tell her as soon as she gets home."

That was tough. Molly didn't have to say it, but she did anyway. "Why did my pet die again?"

I tried my best to be there for her, and William, too, as Ted had been there for me. Not long after that, Molly wanted to try again to find a dog that would sit on the couch while she knit. She was a year older, in fourth grade and in a knitting club at school. This time I looked for the dog Molly described from pets she had seen in real life and in pictures. I got some tips from friends who had paid for their dogs and started a search for a Maltese. Within a month I found what we were looking for - a three-month-old Maltese female for a mere $500 that could be delivered to us in Duluth. Before we said yes, for sure, the breeder offered us the opportunity to meet our puppy since she was making a trip to Duluth for another delivery and said she could easily bring our puppy along for the ride. If we wanted her, she was close to being old enough for us to take her, and if not, we could take a pass.

I actually fell for that! What a sucker! That's the oldest closing technique in the world! It worked. From the moment we saw our tiny girl puppy and Molly holding that little peanut of a dog in her two cupped hands, we were taking her home. Molly snuggled her wee bundle into a pink blanket in her lap. There they were, peaceful, Molly smiling, strapped in a seat belt in the back of the car. I wrote the check, listened to some instructions for our first trip to the vet and excitedly hustled us down the road, heading north for home. The hour passed quickly as we talked about names and all the things we needed to do to welcome Molly's new dog to our family.

Despite William's passionate pleas for a name that in some way went with Cocoa, like "Marshmallow" or "Cookie," Molly had her heart set on "Princess." That was almost too much for William but having observed the Universe's random cruelty in the dog and pet loss department, William put his wishes aside, and genuinely got behind the name, and anything else he could do to make this a winner for Molly. The girls hardly moved from the couch that whole first evening. Princess was so very small that I worried about her at the same time that I thought she was a natural for Molly's sit and stay requirements. I hoped so. I just wanted my little girl's dreams to come true.

Princess delivered. She was the willing recipient of hours of cuddling and petting, especially when she was so little and described by our vet as "never really an outside dog." Molly adorned Princess with everything bling: necklaces, hair bobs, ribbons, and hair clips from her personal jewelry box. It was as it should be from my point of view. Besides William and I were used to bling as founding members of Molly's entourage and fan club over her 7 years of Jazz and Tap dance recitals. We happily provided exceptional care and pampering fit for royalty so that Princess wanted for nothing. Her bed, her blankets, her food and water bowls were pink. Her collar was a Zsa Zsa Gabor diamond choker. Her leash was pink with bling and her coats and sweaters were stitched with bling thread and embroidered for maximum sparkle.

Cocoa was nonplussed by all the hoopla, pleased that as Princess grew, she was company for him. I always felt so much better when we three left for the day in Duluth knowing Cocoa and Princess had each other. Not true to our vet's prediction, Princess grew to be quite the outdoor dog. She and Cocoa ran paths into the grass chasing each other around the cabin. Princess held her own on any hikes and cross-country ski treks we took; and what I loved the most, she kept Cocoa young. He was fit and strong thanks to her morning nudges and noises, "Get up old man," making sure they both went out for an early run. When Cocoa had obliged her silliness and activity, he would direct one bark her way. Princess respected his wishes, having learned the boundary between fun and being a nuisance. She didn't pout or walk away dejected. She simply trotted to a nearby spot in the sun, finding her own place to nap where they could both keep an eye on each other.

Princess and Cocoa completed our family, five beings who lived on the North Shore, who took road trips together, who sometimes broke away for our own individual adventures, but for three sweet years all returned at the end of the day to a place of complete safety and plenty of love.

September came and the new school year was in full swing with everyone happy to have the routine that brought challenging classes, renewed friendships and new activities. During the school week we tried to be home by 7:00. On this particular day we were home by 6:30 happy to have a little extra daylight. Now I wish it had been pitch black because for William and me in the front seat, there was no mistaking Princess lying out-stretched on her side in the dirt, pebbles and bits of grass that made up our driveway. Molly was in the back seat without that view and probably didn't even register that there was only Cocoa's bark greeting us.

Was she napping? Was she hurt? It didn't seem reasonable to even think, "*Was she dead?*"

"Molly, time to get out. Princess might be in trouble," I said as we all got out and hurried over to see Princess only to discover that she was dead. We had knelt down around her, each one looking at her. She wasn't breathing.

"Is Princess dead?" Molly asked.

Wanting to say anything other than yes, I whispered, "Yes. Oh Molly, I am so sorry."

I wanted to put my arms around Molly and hold her, but she burst into tears and ran into the cabin. I understood running. It was just too much.

"Go with her, William," I said, while I grabbed for my phone. I took a dozen pictures of Princess, especially her mouth which appeared to have been foaming. There was a light colored, dried vomit or some other substance in the fur on her chin and on her lips. There were no other signs of injury - no bites, no misshapen legs, no blood anywhere. Her head was fine, her curly white coat unruffled. From the moment I saw her up close, I thought she had been poisoned. What else could it be? She and Cocoa lived in this yard day in and day out, healthy, safe, in the routine of our family, thriving in each other's company. The forest was not a source of danger to our dogs, rather it was their outside kingdom during the days of the year that we didn't have winter. Something had to have come into their space and attacked Princess. I suspected our neighbor Angus. Princess was poisoned. I am sure Angus killed her. I can't prove it. I just think he was a cruel, sick bastard who had to get even. I never spoke to him again. It had been less than a month since I had confronted him.

I didn't think to delay burying Princess so I could actually take her to our vet. Instead, I hoped that documenting what I could see would be enough to learn if she had been poisoned. I was furious as I transitioned to the most important person at that moment, Molly, trying to let go of my all-consuming desire to tear Angus's head off. Like Lake Superior's storming waves of fury that could mercilessly pound the rocks, the waves of anger inside me were building too, and yet they had to wait. I headed for the cabin taking deep breaths.

I was proud of William who sat by Molly on the living room couch as she sobbed. Her face was completely wet, her eyes looking up at me, searching my face for an answer, asking without words, "Why is this happening?" I had nothing to say. I sat next to Molly, sliding her onto my lap so I could comfort her while she cried. William, a shade paler, headed out the door without a word. It wasn't necessary. We both knew he was going to dig a grave for Princess. In time I said,

"Molly, I am going to go and get Princess' best blankets so we can hold her in our arms and carry her outside. William is making a perfect spot for her. Do you want to come with me?" I asked, "Or do you want to stay inside a little longer until we are ready?"

"I'll come with," Molly whispered.

Off we went to swaddle Princess after we had taken off her Zsa Zsa collar. She wasn't that heavy, and Molly had often carried her so when we rounded the corner where Snickers was buried, I asked her if she wanted to hold Princess to say good-bye. Molly snuggled Princess in her arms long enough to say,

"Princess, you were the best dog, and I love you. Thank you for being just my dog and for being so pretty. I'm sorry you died. I miss you so much. I'll never ever forget you because you were my friend, my sleeping buddy, and you made me so happy."

Around about this point in Molly's remembrance, Princess started to get heavy. She wasn't stiff like a board, but she wasn't conforming herself to Molly's arms and body either. Molly paused because Princess was slipping, so I risked cutting Molly off and asked William if he wanted to say anything while I helped Molly pass Princess to me.

"Good-bye Princess," William began. "We will all miss you. I'll try and explain to Cocoa that you are still around, but in a different way. Cocoa and I will take care of Molly, so you can rest now, right here on the top of the hill. We will come and visit you. You were a great dog."

"What will we do without you Princess?" I added. "You were a big part of our family, even though you were the littlest. We will always remember how you jumped and ran and played with everyone from the day we brought you home. Thank you for being such a good friend to Molly and to Cocoa, too. You made our family work so that no one was left out or without a friend. You will always be safe in your spot here with us, and you will always be in our hearts. I love you, sweet Princess."

We spontaneously huddled in for a group hug. When Molly let go, we all did, and I knelt down to place Princess in her grave. There were lots of tears while William gently covered her with dirt and stuck her homemade cross in the ground. We added wildflowers from the woods and hung her little collar on the cross. When there was nothing else to do, we held hands and made our way to the cabin, still crying, still hardly believing what had just happened.

The next morning, I called St. Peter's, the children's school, to get the message to Molly's teachers that Princess had died. As soon as the school day started, Molly was swept up in the love and caring of her classmates and teachers. They were so gentle, understanding and respectful in the way they talked with Molly, so she wasn't alone all day with her loss.

Angus continued to take his spot at the top of our hill on our property line, so we saw him every morning holding his Maltese, a Princess look-alike. I was not able to prove Princess was poisoned, although I tried toxicologists, our vet, the Humane Society and the school of Veterinary Medicine at the University of Minnesota Duluth. I didn't have a sample of the stuff around her mouth before we buried her. Without it, there was only speculation and nothing to analyze other than the pictures which weren't enough. Molly survived, and so did every other dog in the North Star Association family that fall. I wanted to lay Angus out like in "Braveheart" when William Wallace was about to be drawn and quartered. I was ready to gut him. Angus hurt my daughter, and I wanted to hurt him back.

I tried hanging onto that feeling, that intense energy that defines anger, but I couldn't live with that kind of hate for very long. As a person in recovery and a student of Twelve Step programs, I knew resentment was poison and taking up space in my life when I needed all of me for so many more important things. I prayed for Angus, turned it over to God and walked a wide path around conversations, people and places that had anything to do with Angus. For William and Molly, I decided to keep my suspicion to myself and leave Angus where he had already earned his place in the "Danger. Don't go there," category.

Losing Princess truly threw us for a loop. As we were moving from numb to acceptance I desperately wanted to comfort my children, of course, and I also really wanted to offer them more. William and Molly were old enough to participate in conversations about being hurt, being unfairly wronged, getting even, forgiveness, letting things go and putting things in the care of a Higher Power. We had done that for many years in age-appropriate ways. They were surviving the experience of abandonment by their dad, so they knew about loss. They were exposed to process from our various therapists helping us heal, plus we talked a lot in our family.

At this particular juncture I felt strongly about guiding them and remember intentionally talking about the idea that hard things happen. Things that can knock us down and take the wind out of our sails temporarily, but no one, *no one*, not ever, could make them feel broken, take away their freedom of thought or permanently hurt them unless they were to give their permission. They had been raised on the principles of AA and Alanon so I added to that Viktor Frankl's story of survival in a Nazi concentration camp, reading selectively from his book, <u>Man's Search for Meaning</u> when he described his realization that no one could take away his power to choose, to think for himself, to believe what he wanted despite the most awful of circumstances. We remembered examples of times they had been bullied or left out, having learned that those experiences didn't have anything to do with them, just another person's lousy choice. They knew how to shake it off as best they could, how to talk about it and befriend each other. As importantly, they knew how to behave differently when they saw someone else getting the business. We laughed about my send off when I dropped them off at school. It was the same good-bye every morning,

"I love you! Have a great day and find some way to be a good friend to someone." Lo and behold they did and would talk about it on the way home,

"Mom, I did something today that I feel really good about," I remember Molly saying in about 4th grade.

"Oh tell me all about it," I responded with genuine enthusiasm and curiosity. "Well, we were out on the playground in a circle - the girls in my class - and one person was making fun of how short a new girl was and that she couldn't play kickball very well. When people started to laugh, I saw her look sad and not okay so I made a joke about myself so everybody left her alone, and we all laughed about me. Then when we went back in, I told her I was glad she came to our school and that she wasn't too short for kickball. I said I'd be her friend. She smiled and

I did too. I know how that feels, and I didn't care about making a joke about myself."

The tears welled up for me as I said, "Awesome, Molly. I'll bet you made her feel so much better when her day was about to be a total bummer. I'm so proud of you. Good job, sweetie."

Then there was the 8th grade Winter Dance to which I was explicitly invited *not* to chaperone by William who was President of the Student Council. I was always looking for volunteer opportunities to chaperon because I could see the kids with their friends, be with other parents and contribute my time. Volunteering was an important way to feel a little better when I was behind on tuition payments, even when both children had generous scholarships. But this volunteer activity was not to be.

"No! No, Mom," said William when I floated the idea. I knew it when I heard it. He meant no.

"How was the dance?" I eagerly asked William on the night of the event when I picked him up at midnight.

"It was great. I think everybody had a really good time. Do you know what I decided to do?"

"No, tell me," I answered.

"There were a lot of my classmates that weren't out on the dance floor having fun with the rest of us. They were just sitting by themselves along the edge of the gym floor. So, I went up to every single person, one at a time, and brought them out and made sure they were dancing and a part of our big group. Nobody was left out and I felt really good about making sure everyone was included."

"Did everybody find a partner?" I asked.

"No. Some people have boyfriends and girlfriends, but mostly we were just all out there asking the DJ to play songs we liked, and everybody danced with everybody."

"You have a big heart, William," I said, "and you are great at thinking of others. It sounds like a blast. I'm proud of you, honey."

Surely, we were on the right track of being good to our fellow human beings. With Angus, we were confronting mental illness and cruel behavior that required a different kind of boundary. I am glad I went to Thea. I am glad I tackled it head on. As a child, mean and hurtful behavior had been confusing for me, and I had struggled with boundaries and low self-esteem.

"Why me? What did I do? Somehow, I caused this. I must deserve this. This is what I get for doing bad things. No, that can't be right. I don't know."

I remembered those old beliefs and didn't want to allow them room to grow when I saw there could be fertile ground in my children's minds. William and Molly were going to learn different lessons, the ones *I* wanted them to acquire, which was one of the best things about being a single parent. I could teach them that when pain came into their lives, blessings and understandings were there, too, as long as we were willing to find them. We practiced that. I now know they have the tools for health and resiliency if they choose them. Over the years I have watched each child confront bad things, experience disappointment or failure, and consistently exercise responsibility for themselves. I have seen them decide what they accept or reject in terms of others' opinions, and I have seen them choose growth and change over blaming or resentment.

At the time of Princess' death, William and I stayed close to Molly, so she was not alone. I found a heart-shaped locket on a chain with room on one side for a picture of Molly and on the other, one of Princess. When I gave it to Molly, she opened the box, then the locket, said, "Oh. Thank you, Mom," and never touched it again.

That was okay - an out-of-touch idea on my part.

William and his girlfriend Suzannah made Puppy Chow, the snack made of chocolate chips, peanut butter, Chex mix and powdered sugar. Molly's eyes filled with tears when William handed her the gallon baggie, hugging her and telling her he was sorry. Puppy Chow was perfect. It helped fill the emptiness that came with losing her puppy.

Molly's tears flowed easily, and she cried for a long, long time. Healing came little-b- little like it always does. It ebbed and flowed like Her Majesty's waves that kept on coming, embracing the shore, washing away our hurts and cleansing our sometimes frail spirits. That magnificent body of water was always there, offering another day of strength and hope just by her presence. We were drawn to her and we sought her out -- grieving, walking in Her water, listening for Her in the night, or awakening to see Her in the full splendor of a sunrise. She taught us that our part was to show up for another day while she fulfilled Her promise that all was well and all would be well.

Chapter 18

The Times They Are a Changing

Our family took its biggest punch to the gut when we drove home from Duluth on a chilly Sunday night in early October, 2008. William was a 17-year-old junior in St. Peter's upper school while Molly was a 6th grader in the middle school. The temperature that night was in the low 50's. The roads were wet because it was still misting after a rainy day. It was windy, too, so we could hear the crashing waves of Lake Superior. And it was dark. It was always dark driving up Highway 61 from Duluth to Two Harbors.

Nothing about the conditions was unusual in any way. Our community of friends and ten years of living at the cabin had taught us to be vigilant and cautious. We were aware that we lived in country that was rugged and could turn raw, so we did our part to stay safe, respecting our environment. We watched for deer in certain places, we carried extra blankets and survival supplies in our car, we drove the speed limit because headlights just didn't give you that much of a picture of what was ahead. Whoever rode shotgun really tried to stay awake to help the driver spot any danger.

This particular night we were arriving home about 9:00. William had called from Suzannah's house in Duluth around 7:30 to say he was ready to come home, several hours later than our end of the afternoon plan. I didn't care. Suzannah's family was a great place for William. They had plenty of what we didn't have - testosterone. Suzannah was the youngest of four. Her mom and dad were still happily married and lived in their first house where they raised their wonderful daughter and three older brothers. Everyone loved to cook, and the boys ate a lot. So, when William said they had made a great dinner and that's why it got so late, I completely understood and was happy he was happy.

Nevertheless, it was late and a school night so I hurried Molly out of the cabin, not bringing Cocoa inside, although I thought about it, but he wasn't in sight, and I knew we would be back in an hour and a half.

Upon arriving at Suzannah's in a timely 45 minutes, William came right out and opened the driver's side door. "Can I drive?"

"Sure," I answered as I hopped out to walk around to the passenger side. We were on the road with a little chatter about how the day was for everyone, and then settled into a happy quiet ride along our familiar route. I tried to stay awake in case a deer ran onto the road, and I did until Larsmont, a town seven miles from Two Harbors, where I drifted off. The lights of Two Harbors awakened me for the last eight miles of our drive.

"Are you doing alright?" I asked William.

"Ya. I'm fine," he answered.

"Well, let me know if you want me to finish it off." I added, knowing he wouldn't. William and Molly thought my driving was the worst. That was no longer as true as when they had formed their opinions, but I knew exactly why they felt that way. Still, I wanted to offer.

I dozed a bit for the last ten minutes of our drive, but as soon as William turned left onto our gravel road which took us one half mile straight up to our cabin on high, I was awake, grateful we were home safely. William put the car in park. Molly had fallen asleep in the backseat, so I got out to awaken her and help her into the cabin. William met me at the back car door.

"Mom, take Molly in the house. I think I saw Cocoa on the highway," he said.

I knew what he meant from his voice and how he was leaning into me. Shock was running through my stomach, my legs and arms, my throat, trying to take hold but being kept at bay because right behind shock was a reality I had come to know - *I'm the mom here, I'm up.*

"Oh no, William," I said. "Okay. I'll be right out."

"Molly, honey, we're home and it's time to come with me and go inside." Although I didn't get much more than an I'm awake moan, I pulled her toward me and wrapped a blanket around her shoulders as we walked together up the two porch steps and to the couch in the living room.

"Just stay here, Molly. I have to help William with something, and I'll be right back. You can fall back to sleep if you want."

Then I grabbed a favorite navy blue and gold St. Peter's blanket from the couch and ran toward the car, pulling the front door behind me. William had turned the car around and I got in. He had his high beams on, so that when we finally reached the bottom of the hill, we would be able to see onto the road. The half mile down our steep road was way too long for either of us, wanting to get to Cocoa as fast as we could, and not wanting to see what we were so afraid had happened. William's car lights shone onto the dark highway and there was Cocoa, in pieces, his unmistakable coat spread out in lumps, the obvious victim of a big overland truck that probably never even saw him.

William started sobbing. "Can you do this?"

"Oh William, of course," I said as I got out of the car. Opening the blanket, I walked onto the highway as far as I needed to in order to be by Cocoa's head. I scooped him up into the blanket like I had scooped him up many times before, but this time he was ten feet long. It was plenty dark, and I am so glad I could only see well enough to make sure I had all of him, tucking the blanket edges underneath him and then gathering it altogether so I could get back to the car. Cocoa was so warm, his blood was sticky on my fingers, and although I couldn't see him, I knew he was safely in my arms. William and I cried up the hill and without speaking knew what to do. We had just buried Princess, Molly's dog, 6 days before.

Within minutes, William had dug a second grave next to Princess, and in our tradition, fashioned a cross out of a wooden garden stake and sticks from the woods. I walked onto the porch, holding Cocoa.

"Molly," I called. "Keep your jacket on and come out to the porch. I need to talk to you. Please come out right away. It is important."

"What Mom? Okay."

"What is that?" she asked, looking at the bundle in my arms.

"Molly, a sad thing happened tonight. Cocoa got hit on the highway while we were picking up William. I think a big truck hit him very hard and I have him here wrapped up in this blanket."

"Oh no," Molly cried, tears running down her cheeks. "Now we don't have any dogs. Where is William?"

"He is in the backyard digging a grave for Cocoa right by Princess. Come on, we are going to bury him now."

We all gathered by the hole. I held Cocoa. William was on my right and Molly on my left. It was just so sad, so dark, so drizzly and cold. The soft lights of the cabin were plenty for us to see what we were doing but no more.

"William, do you want to hold Cocoa or say anything," I said as I turned to see my 6'3" little boy, hunched over, head hanging down. Stillness. He shook his head no.

"Molly, do you want to say anything?" I asked, hoping she wouldn't flip into funeral mode at which she had become accomplished, particularly when words were required at the side of the grave. I just didn't think William could take it, but I had to ask her.

"I love you Cocoa," Molly said softly. "I know you were William's dog, but I loved you too and I am sorry you got hit."

And then it was my turn. "Bless you dear Cocoa. You were the best dog to all of us and we will miss you so very much. We will never forget you and Princess. Thank you for being in our family, for protecting us, for saving William's life when he needed a friend. No one but you could have brought so much love and comfort. We are so lucky to have been your family. Be still and rest in peace and know that we love you."

And with that I knelt down in the dirt and set Cocoa into his sweet grave. William covered him with dirt and used the shovel to fashion a dome on top of the ground before he put the cross at the head of the grave and gave it a few whacks to pound it in.

"Good-bye Cocoa," we each said as we walked toward the cabin in silence and in tears.

Molly slept in my bed that night. But before I crawled in with her, I sat by myself on the couch in the living room, wrapped in a blanket, numb. I couldn't go to bed when I could hear William crying himself to sleep. And so, I didn't. I stayed for a long time until there was only William's breathing, crying softly to myself, aching a mother's ache, knowing I had nothing; nothing to take away what my children were feeling.

In the quiet, I placed Molly and William in God's hands and I let myself join the night I knew was around me - Her Majesty, Lake Superior, the sky, clouded over and misting, and the earth, within and upon which we rested, grateful for the beauty and peace that cradled all of my family.

The death of both our dogs within a week's time changed our family. Life in our cabin wasn't so idyllic anymore. There was a lot less cuddling going on. Silly and giggling took a hit. There was too much room on the couch when we watched a movie. But most of all, it was just too quiet. Our greeting committee was no longer waiting for us to pull in every night with jumps and barks and kisses followed by racing in the yard. I noticed the children and I each went our separate ways in the cabin, which we usually did having chatted all the way home, but this was different because we were short on companions, and none of us could fill the hole for the other when it came to our dogs.

I wished I had learned to play the trumpet, like my brothers. I was a pianist who often played William and Molly off to sleep. But these nights I really wanted to step out on the back deck and play TAPS.

Cocoa and Princess were our last dogs. William was a year away from college, and Molly threw herself into ballet. The paw prints our dogs left on our hearts were too big to fill right away. No one even suggested a new member of the family. It seemed to me that adulthood was approaching very quickly all of a sudden and that my children were on the verge of venturing out with lessons and truths about love and loss. Sometimes they were loved unconditionally and sometimes they were not. How they would deal with that reminded me of one of my dad's favorite excerpts from Teddy Roosevelt's speech, The Man in the Arena.

"It is not the critic who counts; nor the man who points out how the strong man stumbles, or where the doer of deeds could have done them better. The credit belongs to the man who is actually in the arena, whose face is marred by dust and sweat and blood; who strives valiantly; who errs, who comes short again and again, because there is no effort without error and shortcoming; but who does actually strive to do the deeds; who knows great enthusiasms, the great devotions; who spends himself in a worthy cause; who at the best knows in the end the triumph of high achievement, and who at the worst, if he fails, at least fails while daring greatly, so that his place shall never be with those cold and timid souls who neither know victory nor defeat."

My dad gave me this when I was in high school, though I don't remember the occasion. What I did know was that it was comforting when things fell apart and I knew I had tried my best. I never thought to pass it on to William and Molly, maybe because I didn't display it - out of sight, out of mind, but more likely because they needed no convincing to give things a try. They risked love, they knew disappointment, they were successful and kind and compassionate, taught in a special way by their dogs and their life experiences as children.

It is hard to say, but it just seemed that when our dogs left us, we could move on too, because we carried what they taught us. This is love. This is what love feels like. There is nothing better. Go on now, give it and find it. It's worth it.

Chapter 19
Lake County Jail

As winters settled in each year, so did my depression. Seasonal Affective Disorder was real for me. The cold temperatures, the shortened day, and northern Minnesota's same latitude as Mongolia, brought few hours of direct sunlight. I could feel myself slipping into lethargy, anxiety and an overall feeling of being stuck. The worst part was I didn't care. I knew from AA and my sponsor that the fastest way out of feeling blue and sorry for myself was to serve others, to find a way to give. I had to admit that antidepressants, fresh air, exercise and enough sleep weren't a winning combination on their own, so I started looking past my own belly button, as my sponsor would say, for opportunities to be of service in my community.

One Sunday in church, our bulletin featured a new plea for help from our local jail. The Lake County Jail was directly across the street from our church and not obvious because the building itself was so beautiful and singularly referred to as the Courthouse. Designed by James MacLeod in Beaux Arts architectural style, it was built in 1906, truly breathtaking with its semi-circular gold dome, steep steps from street level to the entrance and its four iconic columns that supported the entry overhang. Inside were the courtrooms and the sheriff's office, *and* the only maximum-security facility between Canada and Duluth. As such, it was important and busy because drugs came across the border, increasing the spread of meth which was surpassing addiction to alcohol, heroin, and cocaine.

The blurb in the bulletin didn't say what kind of help was needed, but I thought I could offer my cleaning skills, envisioning myself buzzing around offices, discreetly improving the work environment. When I went to interview, we never got to cleaning. I met with Toni who coordinated everything that the inmates experienced while they were serving their sentences. For 90 minutes she talked to me about the quality of the prison experience, the population, recidivism, how young so many were at the time of their arrest, and how she wished she could bring something of value to their lives while they were locked up or for sure, she would be seeing them again.

I was so excited listening to her because I was an alcoholic and knew addiction and recovery in my own life. I was a former trainer who specialized in Management and Organizational Development in the corporate world of Honeywell. I *loved* problems! I had earned a reputation for taking on dysfunctional work groups, getting to the bottom of their issues, discovering new options, introducing choices, responsibility and accountability. I was an expert in goal setting, strategic thinking, time management, risk analysis, budgets, cash flow management! *Everything* these inmates needed. I honestly couldn't think of any reason why the curriculum I had designed for Honeywell managers wouldn't be perfect for them, too.

To this day I don't know why Toni trusted me to give it a try. But she did. We offered a weekly, 90-minute, Saturday morning class called "Life Skills." The plan was to meet over a six-month period because that was the average stay of those jailed in Lake County. Our goal was simple: to send every inmate who wanted it out into the world with a plan for survival and success that excluded illegal options and/or a return trip to Lake County.

I was on fire! I couldn't wait to get started. I never stopped long enough to be scared, although the few people I told were in fits about all kinds of potential issues.

"Are you going in there alone?"

"What if they don't give a rip?"

"Can they read?"

"What if they can't read and how about this ...what if they don't know how to write? You know a pencil can be a weapon."

"Will they know where you live?"

"What if they try to hurt you?"

I was too busy pulling all my teaching outlines and getting ready for my first class to listen to much of that. I stopped sharing my news. The facts were that I didn't know what would happen, but I did know what I was going to teach - excellent material, concepts and ways of thinking that I thought were so amazing, I couldn't imagine anyone being bored or wishing to return to a life of crime once they had other options!

I told William and Molly where I would be gone Saturday mornings from 9 to 11. They were happy to have a sleep-in morning so Friday after dinner, I loaded the car with my portable flip chart stand, flip chart paper and magic markers, and my reference materials, Viktor Frankl's <u>Man's Search for Meaning</u>, Stephen Covey's <u>The Seven Habits of Highly Successful People</u>, <u>The Big Book of Alcoholics Anonymous</u> and Thorndike Barnhart's <u>Comprehensive Desk Dictionary</u>. I followed the instructions for jail volunteers and dressed simply - black jeans, white socks, and tennies which I knew would be left at the door. I had a white long-sleeved tee and purple button up cardigan that I thought was appropriate in that it wasn't a low neck or suggestive in any way. Simple jewelry - small pearl studs, and my watch.

The drive from our cabin into town went quickly. I arrived at the Courthouse one half an hour early as instructed with my stuff in a big, green and white-striped, canvas satchel looking a little overloaded with the additional flip chart and rolled-up flipchart paper. But I tried to think small and compact, walking at a quick pace as if everything was under control. Well, everything wasn't. When I buzzed the first "doorbell" to enter the jail, the buzz that came back allowed the door to click open, beckoning me to enter, but not for very long and I missed my opportunity. It took me four more attempts to get the buzzes going back and forth and the door to open by pulling on it at just the right time as I balanced the flip chart and flip chart paper at an angle that would get me through the door. Good grief! Finally! But what did I care? I was in and there was no one around who would have seen that. Actually, upon further reflection, it occurred to me, there were probably cameras everywhere. Still, I didn't have time to worry about that. I had more doors to conquer! The next door with the same buzzer system was up two flights of stairs and opened into what looked like an air traffic controller work area. In the middle of a circular room and on a raised level were three police officers seated at desks in a dimly lit plexiglass bubble talking to different inmates over microphones while they managed their phones and security systems. Toni had been called to an emergency situation I learned from a note on the door so there was no one to say, "Good Morning, Annie. We've been expecting you." Nope, just three separate intertwining conversations allowing me to get the gist of what was going on while I cooled my jets and accepted that my only job was to listen and watch for the time being.

    The conversations stopped and an Officer Lind looked through the glass at me. We nodded at each other. I could see past him and the other officers into the cells where the inmates lived. There were bunks, a TV bolted and chained to the wall way up high at ceiling height, and a table and chairs in the middle of the room and that was it. The lighting seemed hazy and sort of green. I figured there must be some control reason for that. Maybe bright sunlight encouraged too much get up and go. Green light or no, get up and go was not the feeling I had standing and waiting … unless it was to get up and go out of there. Anyway, the officer finally greeted me and added,

    "You know, a 'Life Skills' class is a good idea. It might make a difference for some of these guys. Toni knows you're here, by the way. She'll be up in a minute to get you started. I'm just going to have you wait right there where you are."

That was fine with me. I actually knew this officer as it turned out. In fact I knew the sheriff and most of his band of merry men. When Toni had given me a tour during my second interview, we stopped in the administrative offices to meet everyone on the force. As soon as we walked into their open plan arrangement of desks and I saw the officers faces I thought to myself, *"Oh God, this gig is about to be over."*

Toni carried on, "Gentlemen, I'd like you to meet Annie McMillan. She's going to do a class on 'Life Skills' for our men and maybe, women inmates."

No sooner had she said my name than there were broad grins and chuckling from the officers.

"Oh, *we* know Annie," said one while another followed with, "Yes, *we* do. We know Annie." I felt compelled to get something out there into space to end wherever Toni's imagination was heading, so I blurted out,

"Yes, nice to see you all again. I have had a ... a few speeding tickets," I earnestly admitted, looking directly at Toni, "and some late-night erratic driving coming back from work in Duluth. I wasn't drunk. I was just exhausted leaving the Greysolon Hotel at 1:00 in the morning after overseeing the weddings there. That was my job. But, thankfully, everyone here on the uh uh Force has been ... has been, uh ... great about coaching me, giving me tickets I have rightfully earned, but mostly ... uh, just not making me feel worse than I already have...uh, in the past ...at times."

That comment may have interested if not completely satisfied Toni, I hoped. In the meantime, the guys were already on a roll remembering the times they had pulled me over.

"Erratic! Geeze, I remember one night picking you up at Knife River and following you for 10 miles. I couldn't believe you made it as far as Two Harbors without killing yourself or ending up in the ditch."

"Oh my God," another officer added, "the night I stopped you, you were all over the road, heading for the median and a soft landing, then all the way across your two lanes and continuing like there was an off ramp on your right - which there was not! But you pulled it out at the last second and were doing alright until the weaving started and you were all over the place again. That's when I pulled you over… and as I remember escorted you home from behind." The other guys were nodding and laughing indicating they knew exactly what their buddies were describing.

"And," added the sheriff, "you hit a few things as I recall. For a while every time I saw you, you were driving a different car." More laughing, more head nodding.

They were right. That was true. As my therapist told me, I had a foot in both worlds in those days. She just prayed I'd be upright the next time I was scheduled. Finally, the laughing subsided; from me, too. I kept what was really going on a secret because I was so embarrassed and disappointed in myself. I had returned to bulimia. When I left the Greysolon hotel in the middle of the night, I got myself home without falling asleep by stopping at the Holiday station and loading up. My front seat was a traveling deli: a large bag of popcorn, two bottles of Diet Coke, Snickers bars, a large cup of cocoa and whatever was in the discounted bakery section. The problem with overeating, and especially a lot of sugar in the middle of the night, was that the sugar blues hit about three quarters of the way home. Hence, the nodding off and driving all over the road. It was embarrassing when they were telling their funny stories. I didn't hold anything against them. I really meant what I said. They watched out for me, they got my attention to clean up my driving, and I am sure, saved more than a few lives in the course of doing their job.

So yes, this morning, the officer behind the glass and I had a past which was one reason I didn't mind waiting in the greenly lit room for Toni. I was happy to have the opportunity to show him that I could follow directions - anything to redeem myself.

Toni appeared within a minute, walked me quickly through the sign-in procedure, showed me how to pass my purse and keys in the drawer that slid under the plexiglass, and led me down the hall through three secured doors to a room where I would meet with my class. The room was small, an odd shape, most closely resembling a rectangle. The longest wall, which was opposite the door through which we entered, was completely occupied with a floor to ceiling bookshelf. It was full, too, with books. I liked that. To my left there were seven folding chairs set up in a couple of rows. To my immediate right was a table with a non-working computer. I noticed there was no paper or printer and certainly no writing instruments, recalling the comment of one of my well-meaning relatives, "Pencils can be weapons, too." The rest of the room was bare except for one framed picture. It was a beautiful Cherokee parable called "The Fight of the Two Wolves Within You." The framed story, exposed with no glass in the frame, was drilled and anchored to the wall so no one would take the frame, I guessed. The story was familiar to me, and I liked seeing it again, just like I liked seeing rows of books.

I took a moment to quickly read it and then was quiet.

"The Fight of Two Wolves Within You"

An old Cherokee is teaching his grandson about life:

"A fight is going on inside me," he said to the boy.

"It is a terrible fight and it is between two wolves.

One is evil - he is anger, envy,

Sorrow, regret, greed, arrogance,

self-pity, guilt, resentment, inferiority, lies,

False pride, superiority, and ego

He continued,

"The other is good

he is joy, peace, love, hope

serenity, humility, kindness,

benevolence, empathy,

generosity, truth,

compassion, and Faith

That Same fight is going on inside you –

and inside every other person, like you."

The grandson thought about it for a minute and then asked his grandfather:

"Which wolf will win?"

The old Cherokee simply replied, "The one you feed."

Detecting some apprehension on my part, Toni broke the silence and encouraged me.

"Just see how it goes, Ann. I don't know how many will show up. Don't take it personally. Oh, and if you need to get out, there's a button on the wall over there behind the chairs that you can push at any time, and we'll come right in."

"Okay. Sure. Thanks," I said as I thought to myself, *"That's a hell of a long ways to go if I need to get out, plus it's on the other side of the people I might need to... Note to self: Make your move early."*

Toni announced over the loudspeaker that "Life Skills" class was going to start in the library for anyone who wanted to attend. I set up the flip chart, put my teaching notes on the computer table and stood by the door so I could greet everyone. I reviewed the rules for volunteers in my mind - no touching, so obviously no handshake to greet people, no use of pencils, pens, markers etc., no paper or reading material from me could leave the library, no shoes, first names only, no disclosing of personal information - phone number, address, email - no contact with inmate or inmate's family between classes. I was ready. I took a deep breath and listened as Toni made the rounds to each of the four units to encourage participation and make sure she didn't miss anybody. "Anyone want to go to 'Life Skills' class?" I heard her call out several times.

I thought I could hear some "nos" but no "yeses." Toni buzzed open the library door, and I was pleasantly surprised to see four men walk in. I said hello and introduced myself to each of them as they sat down all in the front row - one next to the other. Toni left and there we were.

Visually, it was a lot to take in the first time. After a while I didn't notice, but that first Saturday there was a sea of orange that was a lot brighter on real people than on actors in a TV prison show. The short-sleeved jumpsuits covered long sleeved Fruit of the Loom-type white cotton tees. They were complemented by prison issue white tube socks and beige slippers. No accessorizing, just individual expression in the form of an abundance of tattoos on all skin that was showing. Heads were an obvious pallet, and some guys pushed up their sleeves to reveal elaborate detail on their forearms.

There sat my first class. Four presentable, very fit, good-looking guys who were missing the Tom Cruise smiles I imagined they must have had at some time. Today they had remains of mouths, teeth and gums ravaged by meth...teeth that were blackened, broken, or just plain gone, chipped teeth surrounded by gums that were scarred from a nasty addiction, its effects on its victims on full display. I couldn't help but feel that there had to be on-going physical pain, too. My heart reached out, and I swallowed hard.

Regaining my focus, I was very aware of the feeling of calm and curiosity in the air. I wanted them to know I was glad to see them and grateful that they would give this class a try. I began by repeating everyone's names a couple of times and said my own.

"I am Annie. I live outside of Two Harbors up the shore a ways. I want to say thank you for coming in here today. Welcome to the Life Skills class which will meet every Saturday from 9-10:30 for the next 6 months or so. Do you mind me asking why you decided to give this a try?" Silence. "Why did you come today?"

Complete silence. Not a word. All eyes focused on the floor in postures that were either sitting and slumped with hands folded in laps, or slumped with legs outstretched, hands folded in laps.

I waited. Ryan started, "I was bored. And there's nothing else to do." Two more followed, "Me too." and "Me too." And the final comment, "I wanted to see what it was about."

"Great," I said, "makes sense to me," and I continued, "I came here today because I am an alcoholic and in the winter I experience bad depression. I was sinking further and further into doing nothing and not caring. That's dangerous because I have two little children who depend on me. I am a single mother. I know enough about addiction to know I was in trouble. My AA sponsor taught me to get up and do something for someone else if I was feeling sorry for myself. Two weeks ago I saw a request in our church bulletin for volunteers at the jail. I clean houses, so I came to meet Toni with my list of clients for references. Turns out she was looking for a different kind of volunteer that actually fit me better. She wanted someone who could bring experiences and learning to you, some classes you could attend that would give the time you are here some value. That's where the idea for this Life Skills course originated.

So, what qualifies me to teach you? Why would you waste your precious time coming in here and listening to me? Well, because I also have a twenty-year professional career in my past at the Honeywell Corporation where I ran the company's University and was a trainer for all levels of management. I love the material that I am going to teach you. It is so powerful. It changed me when I first learned it, and now I love passing it on. I am ready to teach you the same life management skills I have taught to the presidents of universities like the University of Minnesota at Duluth, or chief medical officers of hospitals like Lake County Hospital, or executives of small and large businesses that you know and that are right outside our doors here. These people are successful because they know some stuff that gives them an advantage, and I see no reason why you shouldn't have the chance to learn that stuff too, so you can have an advantage."

They were listening, not fidgeting, sort of making eye contact. But I thought they were with me, so I took a deep breath and continued, "Here's what I am not. I am not a therapist. I am not a doctor. I have no authority over you. I am not associated with the judicial system in any way. I have nothing in my power to make you stay here or come back or leave and never come back. It is okay whichever way it goes. I'm selfishly here for me, to keep myself sober and sane. And I'm here with something to teach that I believe in. Any questions?"

Complete silence. "Anyone want to leave?" More silence with some head shaking no and one verbal,

"Nope."

"Okay, "I said with a big smile and a sigh of relief, "then let's get started. Who knows what a paradigm is?" I wrote the word on the flip chart and when no one answered, I handed Ryan my dictionary and asked him to look it up. We were on our way.

For the next several years I taught a men's class every Saturday morning and started a women's class shortly thereafter that met on Wednesday nights. It was a ball. I cannot begin to describe how much fun we had, from the moments of absolute confusion to mornings of embarrassment when I wanted to push the button, to sheer outbursts of joy when someone had a breakthrough or shift in their self-image. I fell in love with my guys and absolutely adored the evenings I spent with the women. It was humbling to work with mothers separated from their babies, mothers who were full of guilt, who had deep desires to have another chance at a life, who knew if they stayed sober, they could raise a good family with or without a good partner.

Interestingly, the men's class wanted to name our class. "Life Skills" wasn't doing it for them. So, wanting nothing but the best for my people, I asked for expertise from a talented friend of mine who owned his own marketing business and with whom I worked at the Duluth Superior Symphony Orchestra. He put me through a series of branding type questions and then sent me back to my students with five possible names for our course and visuals to brand it. The guys loved the whole process and chose "The Sequel" for the name of our work plus a rising sun for our symbol.

I shared the idea with my women's class who were far more irreverent about the whole thing and named their work "NoMoHo" epitomized by a strong woman in a stance with arms crossed in an "X" like the symbol for poison. They thought that up on their own and never wanted input from an advertising executive. They got my vote!

After the first six months I had a pretty good idea of the actual course curriculum, assignments, logistics, what *not* to do, and how to handle turnover. When I was able to see a person in class over a six-month period, which was most of the time, that inmate was able to walk out of the jail with a plan in their hands, a decent-looking document, that led to a place to live, transportation, a guaranteed job opportunity, a budget, and a community of people in place to love them, support them in their sober journey and keep their days of incarceration in the rear view mirror. They often had their parole officer with whom they also met on a regular basis, plus the memory of a sendoff by men or women who believed in them and wanted them to succeed.

I was instructed *not* to see any of my graduates again. Any follow-up required a formal meeting specifically scheduled in the courthouse to discuss their plan and only their plan. No socializing. As a teacher, I wanted to know how my students fared when their plans met reality. But that never happened. For a jailed person who completed their sentence and moved on with a head full of steam to start over, the last thing they wanted to do was spend time traveling to the courthouse in Two Harbors. I understood. What did happen was letter writing between the women and me. Every so often I would get mail forwarded from the jail, a letter written on lined paper ripped from a three-ring notebook, both sides of the paper filled with news, or a store-bought card with all blank surfaces filled. The updates from the women were positive and honest about their struggles and successes. Each one who wrote was making progress, putting in the work to honor their commitment to live a sober and clean life. I loved writing back, relishing their stories and sending my love, never excluding the heartache I experienced from missing each of them in my life.

Chapter 20
Rhoda

Rhoda and I communicated the most. Besides being my most frequent repeater in the Two Harbors Jail, she bounced around to different rehab centers for ten years until she made it out of the hell of a life she lived until age forty. At maybe 100 pounds, Rhoda was tough; tough like gristle in steak. She was an extrovert, blond and fidgety, and pretty in a beat-up sort of way. A handful of guys had chosen to leave their calling cards in scars on her face, arms and hands which most days she made the effort to cover by pulling on the long sleeves of her prison issue.

Rhoda had an unmistakable, raspy laugh and a ready smile. Sure, she was missing some teeth, and parts of her body were always hurting but that didn't stop her from wanting a life. She had no children, just a brother in Duluth who wanted nothing to do with her, and a boyfriend, Tyler; "abusive Tyler" we called him, to whom she returned where she hit bottom after bottom after bottom of alcohol and abuse. Tyler's idea of a welcome home party took place deep in the woods northwest of the town of Finland, Minnesota in his trailer home, where he busted up her fragile sobriety, raped her, mercilessly beat her and dumped her outside naked, locking the door behind him as he stumbled back inside to sleep it off. With new cuts and bruises, cold and starving, Rhoda somehow survived the days that could turn into weeks until Tyler let her back in.

Because Rhoda received assistance from a variety of agencies in at least three counties, she bounced around, and we would lose touch. Her preferred consequence for bad behavior was without question, six months in the Lake County Jail, a small price to pay for safety and time to heal. But she didn't always luck out. Some of the places that picked her up did her more harm than good. On one occasion she wrote to tell me she was in Duluth pleading with me to come visit before she went crazy. With mixed feelings, I went to see her at Duluth Bethel, a combination halfway house, treatment center and residential facility. Relieved to hear that she was okay, I was eager to visit, to provide support and friendship, despite my understanding of the Lake County jail guidelines to which I had agreed. I knew I wasn't supposed to see her. In addition to that I knew Rhoda was a skilled manipulator, and I didn't want to be used to enable her. Still, I decided to go.

    Duluth Bethel sprawled up the side of a steep hill the length of a whole city block. Overlooking Lake Superior at the southern entrance to the city of Duluth, the facility was built of huge, reddish-brown stones with a few small windows, depressingly reminiscent of a 19th century insane asylum or some other place I imagined a person might go in and never come out. The entrance on the side of the building was a regular-size door, totally out of proportion and not convincing as a statement about security, despite the fact that it was decorated with locks and buzzer systems. When prompted with the right codes and responses, this outer door opened into a small space with another door covered with locks and buzzer systems. Then, just like other old institutions, the final door opened into a space where hallways converged in an atmosphere that smelled unmistakably of bleach and the latest institutional cleaner. Cold and damp, I wished I had thrown on a sweater. Mundane sounds echoed down the halls of the low-lit structure built of more stones. No hope blossoming there.

    Still Rhoda never gave up. With each incarceration she would denounce the terrible life she had as an addict, including her life with Tyler which she knew was likely to kill her if she went back anymore. Despite the depressing nature of Bethel, it was great to see her and listen to her half hour of complaining about the staff that stole her stuff and knocked her about on occasion. Bottom line she was hanging in there, serving her time. I was glad I had gone to see her.

After her three to six months, or whatever it was this time, I learned that she was released to the streets. I also learned that eventually she ran out of everything she needed to live and called Tyler to take her back.

The bottom Rhoda continued to scrape never changed. I think it was just the repetition of abuse that finally got through to her. The last time I heard from her, she had a new boyfriend, three years of sobriety and a routine in her life that had new characteristics, safety and health. I was immensely happy for her, so grateful, so humbled by the phenomenon of addiction and recovery, and how by the Grace of God, so many of us were given a second chance. I was happy Rhoda and I had a connection when we first met in my women's class. I was glad I visited her in various shelters, arriving with her requested treats, hair dye and chewing gum. I was gratified that I had made the effort to bring her friendship when she was failing in her early attempts to get out of a life that was killing her. Finally, I was glad for the experience of having gone out of my way many times, not knowing if it would make a difference. Many people had helped me and I had the sense that Rhoda was there for me to pass it on, arriving in my life at a time when I could help another alcoholic. She was consistently burning bridges, so in a way, I wasn't surprised to hear from her when she would show up in desperation with the crisis of the moment.

"Ann, Rhoda. Listen, I'm in a mess. My brother kicked me out and I have all my belongings in 20 cardboard boxes. Could you keep them for me for a little while, just until I can find a place?"

"Ann, Rhoda. Say, I have a place to live but I have to leave my boxes at another place so could you bring the boxes? I've gotta get in them and then I can take you to the place where I can leave them. And then I just need a ride to my new place. It's all in Duluth."

I never had the full picture. All I know is that she didn't give up, so neither did I. I read Rhoda's letter one more time, folded it and put it back in its envelope with a sense of gratitude and peace. She made it.

In another case, I stayed in touch with a woman named Janine, who wrote to ask me if I could come to see her, just to say hello while she was working at her new job at Walmart in Duluth. I responded, "Of course! Send me the details," honored that she wanted to share her post-jail life with me. Our time was short because we didn't want to detract from her doing a great job. But, for five minutes the focus was all about congratulations, smiles, and hugs, her put-together clothing, her unmistakable sense of pride and that center-stage moment to show that she made it. She was beautiful. It was like having another baby for me. We both cried, waving happily as she went back to work and I, out the door, "You've got this, Janine!"

The connections with my students in the women's class got deep very quickly. I never knew what their weeks between classes were like because we were not there to discuss that, although from their random comments, I knew their experiences were different from their male counterparts. They each occupied a single cell or shared a cell with one other inmate, for example, plus arrangements to see their young children seemed to be a higher priority. What I did know was that once our class started and we took a couple of deep breaths together, it was time to get real. There were few barriers between any of us. We were interested in each other's problems - children, abusive husbands, no money, no jobs, addiction and now jail. But more than that we huddled in a safe space where we shared energy of compassion, love, encouragement and laughter, female nourishment that was so potent in the face of miserable situations.

One Wednesday evening before Thanksgiving Day in my second year of volunteering, I asked for permission to bring in a tablecloth and five pencils for use during one exercise. Toni said that would be okay, so I rounded up the pencils, and then picked a square cloth that had lace and embroidery on each of the corners. It was a heavy, light beige cotton, one of my favorites given to me by my mom. After introducing the topics of acceptance and gratitude at the start of our class, we talked about the reality of being in the Lake County jail that night. We explored the power of gratitude and its ability to shift your whole being no matter what external circumstances were present. I asked the women to write what they were grateful for despite their incarceration or maybe even including their incarceration. I made a list, too.

When they had finished, I asked them to help me set up a table that we could gather around with our lists. We removed the non-working computer from the one table in the room to a place on the floor, making a new place for the table in the center of our space. We put enough chairs around the table for all five of us. I put the tablecloth on it, squaring it perfectly and pressing out the crease marks. It changed our place, and we knew it as we sat down together. It felt good, a little risky, but mostly right to be one - women together - in a Thanksgiving eve sort of way.

I asked them if they were alright with holding hands for a short prayer. They were quiet as they nodded, so I spoke quietly, too, "Be present here O Lord, Great Spirit and Creator. Bless our friendships, the generosity of our hearts and our desires to make good lives happen for ourselves, our families and each other. In gratitude we come together tonight. Amen."

After a little squeeze of our hands, we began, each one taking time to talk about their Thanksgiving memories and to read their gratitude lists. God was present that night, like I always knew he was whenever I went to the jail. That night was a holy space, and I don't think any one of us left that room unmoved, concretely reminded of all the good in our lives and the power of giving thanks.

Chapter 21
More Jail and Sean

As far as my men's class was concerned, I had an entirely different variety of experiences in and out of the jail. Not surprisingly, there were always more men inmates than women, so it seemed predictable that there were more chances for things to go wrong, at least regarding jail protocol. Generally, I had seven or eight men per Saturday class which was a "full house" in our library meeting room, compared to three or four women on Wednesday nights. If I tried something with the men, who were a more challenging class, and it worked, I carried that lesson plan over to the women's class.

As a professional educator, I was most familiar with student groups of 10 to 35, so having a class of 7 was a change I welcomed. I looked forward to hearing from everyone when I was presenting new ideas. As far as introducing material or discussing a concept, I had the flip chart, different colored markers, well prepared notes and organized references at my disposal. My tools worked well in the space and my students were attentive, so that class management wasn't a problem. There was no shortage of unpredictable participation which kept it interesting for all of us. In most ways, at least ways that were important to this class, we were all new to each other, our personal stories and thoughts. Based on their reactions in class, I concluded not much of that kind of thing was ever shared during their time in the general population. I understood. It could lead to vulnerability which was not a good thing.

Our 90-minute classes flew by each week. If my students weren't chiming in with their opinions, there was the constant activity of reading a passage or a quotation in addition to looking up words in the dictionary so that we all were on the same page. Realizing on day one that I had no idea if anyone could read, or spell or speak English or other languages, I was bound and determined to not have judgments about those things derail my class. I asked all my questions with the same tone as if to say, "Just fact finding here."

"Do you read, Al?"

"Well, sort of."

"Awesome. Have you ever used a dictionary?"

"Nope."

"No problem. Do you know what a dictionary is for?"

"It is for words, I think."

"Yes, exactly. Who has used a dictionary?" Hearing "I have," from John, I continued, "Great. John? Here, come and take this dictionary and explain how it works."

John took the dictionary and did a great job of show and tell, explaining in his own words, the alphabetical arrangement of thousands of words and how the definitions, parts of speech, alternative meanings etc. followed. I reinforced the main points and then asked John and Al to work together, to find and read to us the definition we needed. To this day I think the best thing I brought into that class was the dictionary.

Because no one was allowed a writing implement with which to take notes or brainstorm their own thoughts on paper before sharing them with the group, I was challenged to find a way to work with each person on their individual lives in the midst of our whole class. I didn't have the luxury of handing out paper and pen so I could ask them as a group to individually record their thoughts. There was no way to create privacy for self-exploration, no other room where I could talk one on one while the rest of the class did something else. There was just the group.

Once everyone appeared to grasp the introductory concepts and indicated that they understood that our goal was a unique plan for each class member, it was time to get personal. It looked to me like we were headed for more of a therapy group than a classroom. I was wary because of the risks I would be asking each man to take as a part of self-disclosure. I was also aware that the whole thing could go belly up for reasons I wasn't even able to contemplate. Still, I felt confident about leading someone through the process for change and equally as sure that they would find great value in the experience if they would stick with it.

I had some ideas and I decided to pray about it asking God for guidance in the words I chose and my demeanor. I was convinced that breaking the chains of recidivism was going to require each man to dig deep and clean out the dark places where their self-esteem had been pummeled growing up. My students didn't have the same histories so speaking in generalities was going to be too safe and ineffective. Unless they could name and grieve their own losses and know the validation and support of our jail family, I thought we would be wasting our time. The time to drill down, one man at a time had come; to take a good look at their individual histories, their current behaviors, their patterns, their world views, their personal stumbling blocks.

And what about my ability? Would I be able to facilitate enough trust building so that the first man in the hopper could return to the general population and not be so vulnerable that he would attract predators? What role would his classmates take on? Could I set someone up for harm without realizing it?

While these were unknowns, I continued to believe we had to go to dark places in order to eventually fill them with light. I was confident in the process. I knew there was risk. This was a spiritual challenge requiring a close walk with my Higher Power, so I opened myself to God's guidance trusting I would know whether or not to proceed each step of the way.

I entered the Courthouse in the following weeks. Once we were settled, I began by reviewing the work from our first classes, which was handy not only for bringing us all to the same place mentally, but because there were new people coming to our class. The word had spread, and it was good! In no time we touched on a welcome, the purpose of the class, the absence of requirements to attend - always your choice - and definitions plus examples of a paradigm, right and left brain thinking, why change happens, and choice - the one thing that makes man different from any other living species. Without prompting, a couple guys volunteered insights from their weeks. Others related or listened respectfully, so fifteen minutes in, I felt validated about the groundwork and ready to begin the formal curriculum for how to create lasting change in each of their lives, relegating Lake County Jail to a memory of the past.

 I started by asking Al, the man closest to me in the first chair of the first row, what he wanted for himself, for his life, to fulfill his dreams, to be happy, to be free. Silence. I figured as much, but I wasn't deterred. I had been there before, so I asked another couple of questions. "What do you like? What do you like to do?"

 "I don't really know," he added, followed by more silence.

 "Well, do you like to eat?" I offered. And then in the midst of chuckling and snorts from the rest of the class, he answered, "Well yeah, duh, I like to eat."

 "Do you eat a lot?" I came right back.

 "Sometimes. It depends. Not the shit in here."

 "Got it," I said as I speed wrote "Eat" on the flip chart. "Well what kind of food? Stuff you cook? Stuff you hunt? Stuff you grow? What your family cooks?"

 "Well, I'm pretty well known in my parts for the best barbecue anybody's ever eaten," he bragged as I thought to myself, *"There it is, like manna from heaven."* "No kidding! So, you know how to cook! Do you like to cook?" I asked, so excited that we were on our way.

 "Yeah, I like to cook very much. I've been to community ed cooking classes, and I worked for a summer with the new chef at the restaurant in Beaver Bay. I woulda kept going but I got busted and I'm here. Wasn't the first time."

From there the conversation for this man expanded and explored all the things under the heading of "What I Want" which I wrote in a bulleted list down the right half of the flip chart paper, taking great care to use exclusively his words, his embellishments, and his examples. I let the momentum in the class build, the chatter and laughter gathering its own speed. We needed to leave those four walls in the worst way and the energy we were creating was our fuel. Other men related stories of their own, making side jokes and taking jabs at each other and sometimes at me. But I didn't care as long as I was coming up with a rich, full description of one man's dreams that maybe even he had never acknowledged.

At about the halfway mark of our time together, I asked a few times, "Is there anything else you want? Did we get it all? This isn't your one and only time to do this, but for now, do you think we have a good start?"

"Yeah, that's good," Al answered. "If I could have that …. whoo…my life would be worth living and I wouldn't spend any more time with you clowns in a place like this." More laughter.

"Okay, I'm with you there." I laughed too. "This is an impressive list. Good for you. First of all, you *can* have it. And the next step to getting there is to get a grip on where you are."

At that point I started another column directly left of the first column and labeled it, "Where I Am." Then we read each bullet on the right and contrasted it with what was real in the moment. The room slowly got quieter as we made our way down the items. With each description of "This is where I am today," I carefully asked follow-up questions like, "Why is that?" "Where did that behavior come from?" "Who taught you that?" "Who told you that?" "How old were you?" "Can you explain more about that?"

As soon as we came to the bullet "I want to be a great father to my kids," followed by my question, "And how are things going now?" the tears began to flow. It wasn't just Al. It was every man. There was so much guilt and sadness surrounding their own children and ultimately the buried pain about themselves as little boys. It was too much to bear without expressions of deep loss. Listening to the stories of hurt and abuse bound us one to another, understanding we were not alone and privileged to know the past of one man's journey and the damaging cruelty that he endured as a child. It was sacred.

We proceeded to build the second column and with ten minutes to go I brought our session to a close. I wanted a few minutes to honor what had happened for all of us that morning, especially Al.

"Thank you, Al, for being the first to talk about your life. It has been a privilege for all of us to be trusted with your story. You have our respect and commitment to keep what is said here protected. I will bring this back to you next week in a cleaned-up format to which you can certainly add if you think of some other things this week. Alright?"

With Al's agreement and seeing nodding heads, I transitioned, "I am excited for next week, because we are going to start to figure out how to get from here (pointing to the "Where You Are" column) to here (pointing to the "What I Want" column). Now here's the secret, it's not that hard and you can do it. No question you can do it! I'll help you. We'll all help you, and then we'll go on and help the next one of us in the same way. Okay. Thank you everyone. Have a great week. See you next Saturday."

After I pressed the button on the wall and an officer came to escort my students out, I rolled up my flip chart paper and headed home, excited to see William and Molly. I was ready to play with them and surprise, surprise, I was not in the least feeling sorry for myself. I had been blessed that morning, and I was pretty sure I had a format that could work.

On Saturday of the next week, I arrived with the first glimpse of the product I was creating for each student. Of course, I only had work documented from one exercise, but it was typed, using some different fonts to set their name apart from the content of their thoughts. I used some different colors too, which added to the interest and professionalism of their document. I brought it to Al in a file folder that was labeled with his first name and in which it would remain until we completed it week by week with all its reference materials, contact information and other relevant details for his success.

I began the class with my usual summary and added that I had been especially busy with our class work, too. When I pulled out the folder and gave it to Al, the smile on his face spread quickly. The other guys got up and peered over his shoulder. They liked it and they especially saw that Al liked it - seeing his own words in phrases that he remembered saying and that were truly his own expression of himself. That was important fuel for the next weeks of work that followed. We developed strategies, defined specific resources, sometimes our ideas required research that could only be answered by people on the outside. We did hard emotional work too, cleaning up some bad behavior and its accompanying guilt with amend making letters, phone calls and written notes or drawn pictures to wives and children whom they would see at visitation. We practiced time management, budgeting, cash flow analysis, planning principles, and cost-benefit analysis. We got good at making lists, prioritizing, re-prioritizing, right next to exploring the power of prayer and meditation as ways to get centered. At every opportunity I brought examples of achievers from all situations, circumstances, backgrounds and races, reading short stories from *The Grapevine*, an AA publication, and other inspirational clippings. There wasn't a class that we didn't talk about self-responsibility and accountability, and how that would be a very different way to live as opposed to looking for someone to use or blame or hide behind.

As the weeks went by, more and more of our class members were somewhere in the process of learning new life skills and creating their individual plans for when they would get out. I found myself relaxed as I went to the class, excited as usual to teach, but not as disciplined about my preparation as a professional. I'll admit to losing my edge, I mean I must have on the Saturday morning I woke up late and was rushing out the door to get to the jail on time. I remember a general flurry of activity before I left the cabin, as I ran to the bathroom, quickly washed my face, pinched my cheeks for color - no time for make-up, brushed my teeth and combed my hair before heading to my bedroom to throw on a clean bra, panties and tee shirt before pulling my jeans that were conveniently sitting on the floor ready for me - right leg, then left. Kissing William and then Molly good-bye, I whispered, "I'm going to teach at the jail. See you for lunch." I jumped in the car, glad I had packed it the night before, and drove safely into town.

I made it with a moment to spare and took a deep breath once I was in the greenly lit outer sanctum, where I attempted to gather myself for the 90 minutes ahead. We got off to our usual good start in class. I was moving between the person who was speaking and the flip chart, writing their thoughts down or flipping to another page to sketch something out and make a new point. I was animated and rarely sat during the class, although there was a chair for me. At times it was right to sit, to be eyeball to eyeball when someone was talking. But this morning, nope, I was on my feet, and we were moving right along.

As I was changing markers to get a new color, I heard what I thought was a giggle or muffled snicker from one of the men… and then another. I looked over my left shoulder briefly as I continued writing. Seeing nothing unusual, I finished my point and turned around to a mix of smiles and looks that clearly conveyed, "Uh oh - something's up…something's up, and you don't know about it."

"What," I said as a statement not a question, looking straight at my class.

More chuckling.

"What is so funny?" I asked opening my hands in front of me while I looked down my front. Were my jeans unzipped? Had I accidentally given myself a mustache with the magic marker?

"What?" I repeated, smiling because they were so goofy, and I wanted to be in on the joke. And then I noticed a small black mound of something on the floor between me and the inmate closest to me, Skeeter, the brightest, naughtiest flirt and funniest person in our class. He was tipped back on two legs of his chair, with his arms crossed and with that know-it-all Eddie Haskell grin on his face. I expected to hear,

"Hello Mrs. Cleaver," but there was only silence and a growing number of grins. Nobody moved and I didn't either at first, asking myself, *"What is that? Is that a small animal? A dead mouse? It's not moving. A sock? It's not big enough to be a sock, but it looks like cloth."* And then, when I couldn't help myself from bending forward to take a closer look, I saw immediately that it was a pair of my black silk panties that had apparently stuck to the inside of my jeans when I had pulled them on that morning, panties positioned to slide right on down and out once I moved about enough.

"Oh, dear God," I thought as I recognized them, deciding to stay locked in my forward position until I had a plan for what to say and what to do. I must have looked like a mime with a problem, although I tried to hurry up and think of something so I could move. Finally, I bent my knees, approached my panties by leaning even farther forward and then with one smooth move, picked them up like a magician where they disappeared in my hand. Feeling the need to speak, I stood up and sort of whispered, "I guess these are mine."

The guys broke out in hysterical laughter with lots of comments. "Where were YOU last night?" "Who was the lucky guy?" "Anyone we know? Try us, we might!" "A little short on the time to get ready this morning? Or did you plan that? You planned that. It's so obvious! You've got a crush on us, Annie."

"Well, that part is true," I laugh with them. "You do know I am fond of all of you. But I really didn't... I accidentally ... oh, forget it."

I couldn't help but join in until the hoopla died down. I am sure I was bright red while they were having a great laugh at my expense which I figured I deserved. I made one more attempt at explaining why I was so tired Friday night falling into bed without . . .without... oh whatever, which was followed by more raucous laughter until we had all gotten it out of our system.

The class finished and it never happened again, but I realized that morning how great it was to laugh - to share a good belly laugh. I had made very good friends who were laughing with me, not at me. At least that's what I wanted to believe. Truthfully, in my gut and my heart of hearts, I knew I had crossed a line. I understood the line and I wanted to ignore the niggling of discomfort in my stomach, but I couldn't. What was there to do? Nothing at this point. It was done. I had crossed a line that was there to ensure my safety and my ability to teach. Men whom I knew well in some ways but not at all in others, now knew me as a vulnerable woman - a place I knew could be trouble.

I was right. Two weeks later when Skeeter got out, he got my phone number somehow and called me at ten at night.

"Annie, this is Skeeter. Would you like me to come over and lick your pussy?"

"No, thank you," I managed to answer and hung up the phone shaking.

I got over Skeeter and his comment. I had learned my lesson. In spite of it all, I continued teaching with results that were satisfying for me and my students. Inmates finished their time and moved on. Other less satisfactory endings occurred because an individual would get transferred to another facility or have to finish out their time in a penitentiary. I hated to "lose" anyone from my class, but I always sent them with as much as we had gotten done for their use down the road.

I decided to believe I was making a difference. But honestly, it was hard to tell what the real impact of my work was because I relied on word of mouth and an occasional unsolicited report from one of the parole officers. Generally speaking, my class was thought of as a plus. My reputation in the Two Harbors judicial circle improved, like that was difficult. I didn't see repeat offenders coming through what used to be called the revolving door: jail in the winter because it was warm with three squares, and the streets in the summer because there was freedom to run scams, be with their people until it was time to design their arrest for the onset of winter.

There was one man in my class who was in his forties, older for sure than most of the guys, but not exclusively. Some of my students who lived a life of crime, considered themselves to be damn good at it and planned on living their lives out that way. This man, Sean, was not like that. He was a gentler soul who was in and out of jail, who attended AA in Silver Bay where he lived and who was a benevolent father figure to the younger guys in the class, offering lessons learned and encouragement. He was a big guy, blond and handsome. From the first class in which he spoke, I felt like he had my back not because of anything he said specifically, but just because he had a certain command of the room that made me feel safe. One Saturday a new inmate came to our class for his first time which I think was within his first 24 hours of arriving at the Lake County Jail. He had the shakes; his eyes were a little on the wild side, and he stood up and sat down a lot, running his tattooed hands up and down his arms in between wringing them. He was detoxing. He spoke in bursts, asking a few disjointed questions in increasing volume as he impatiently waited for answers. Wanting to give him options and pretty convinced that today was not going to work out well for him, I said, "Jerry, I am glad you are here, but if you are not hearing what you want you don't have to stay. Maybe this just isn't working for you today. We'll be here next week, and you are welcome at any time. What do you think? Would you like to stay or go on back to your cell?"

He was agitated and fidgeted even more at which point Sean stood up, pushed the button and slowly moved toward Jerry presenting a formidable presence in a small space. Everyone stayed seated. It was quiet. The door buzzed, and as it opened, Sean said, "Jerry would like to go back to his cell." Jerry moved toward the guard and that was that. Nothing was said, and I continued with the class.

Brief encounters like that were cause for a burst of fear every now and again. They would occur and then they would pass. They were unexpected. They were isolated and cushioned with weeks of smooth sailing before and after, so they seemed to me more the rare exception than the rule. I chose to understand them as opportunities to be grateful for protection from my Higher Power, and therefore, an opportunity for an on-the-spot silent prayer of thanks. I had long believed in angels and there were just too many good endings to close calls to relegate my situations to good luck. I found that the fear wasn't in my control, but my reaction to it was. It never grew into an issue. I loved my experiences at the jail and never reached a point where I felt a need to stop because I was not safe or without options.

One day in the fall when our firewood was running low, I returned home at the end of the day to find a cord of split logs in a big pile - not stacked, just unloaded right there in our front yard. No one was in sight, and I hadn't heard from any of the foremen of the North Star Association who perhaps knew the children and I were low on wood. I was elated *and* puzzled, really grateful for such a wonderful surprise. A day or two later, Sean from my jail class called to say hello and to ask me if I had gotten the wood. I don't know how he knew where I lived nor do I know how he or Skeeter got my phone number. I did know he had completed his jail sentence because he was no longer in class and as far as I knew was back to life in Silver Bay. I hadn't seen him for a couple of months, nor did I expect to. I missed having him in the class.

"Sean, was that from you? Thank you so much! How did that happen? Where did you get it? Do I owe you some money?" I babbled, so happy to hear his voice.

He laughed and answered, "I log up here and I know a lot of people who cut wood so I thought you might need a load for winter. I didn't have time to stack it. I had to get the truck back, but I could help you with that this weekend if you would like."

"That would be great," I said dismissing any intention of being true to my agreement with Lake County Jail. "Any time Saturday afternoon would work. I'm done with our class at the jail by 11:00."

"Okay, I can be there more like 2:00," he said.

"Great!" I said and we ended with good-byes and a "See you then."

I was excited and really touched, too. I had been told by one of the officers at the jail that Sean's family of origin was full of alcoholism and that he was the only one who was sober. He took responsibility to care for his parents and I knew he wasn't married but instead stayed close to his family that needed him. Sean had the build of a logger, who spoke of uncles and cousins somewhat, but mostly seemed to be living simply with the right idea for a sober life. When he arrived on Saturday we got right to it, stacking the wood in the woodshed and in smaller piles around the house when we needed more room. I didn't invite him to come in because it didn't seem right. The jail rules were in the back of my mind, but honestly, I just didn't want them to apply to me that day. As the early sunset arrived with its chill in the air, we were finishing up with the wood, when I said, "Sean, would you be willing to help me with one more thing before you go? I mean if you have time?"

"Sure," he responded, "What is it?"

"Well, I have this large bureau that I bought at an auction for my daughter's school, St. Mark's Lakeside School in Duluth. And I have wanted to bring it into my cabin so I can use it. It is down the road at my mother's place, and I just don't have the strength to move it myself."

"How far away is it?" Sean asked.

"Oh, just a mile and a half. The dresser is on the first floor of a cabin there. It shouldn't be difficult. It is just heavy - it's a two-person job."

"Alright. Sure, I can help you with that," said Sean as we walked toward his truck.

I checked my watch for the time, aware that I had to leave for Duluth by 5:00 to get William and Molly. It was still early, so I relaxed on the drive, saying little more than, "Thank you so much for helping me with this," to which Sean answered, "Sure."

This cabin of my mother's was dimly lit at best even when it was fully occupied, relying on floor and desk lamps to light up jigsaw puzzles, games of Hearts or reading a book by the fire. With no one staying there, the breaker switch for the lights was off, so it was a little bit difficult to see. I thought about walking the length of the cabin to where the breaker box was located but decided instead to just hurry and make the most of the waning afternoon light.

"Sean, follow me," I began, "We just have to go to the far side of this room and move a couple of end tables. Then we can get to the dresser."

It never occurred to me that Sean might not be used to being around fine pieces of furniture where surfaces could be scratched, and dings were to be avoided. But I noticed too late, that perhaps that was the case. I tried to help in order to avoid more bumps and gouges, saying nothing because I couldn't think of anything to say that wouldn't potentially hurt his feelings.

Out of the quiet Sean spoke. He was slightly behind me on my left so I couldn't see his face, but his voice was deep and clear.

"Annie, may I ask you something personal?"

My heart stopped a little and I answered, "Yes, sure."

"Do you have a boyfriend?"

I almost giggled. I was so relieved. I don't know what I thought he was going to ask me, but it wasn't that!

"No, I don't," I answered.

"Would you like one?" Sean spoke next.

"I'm not sure," I said slowly. "I think so."

It was so quiet. As much as the light allowed us to see, I looked at Sean, and he looked at me. Neither of us said anything else. We just stood there.

Someone broke the silence, probably me, and we started speaking again, but now about the moving logistics of the bureau, taking drawers out first, removing the mirror as it was suspended between two carved pieces of wood above the bureau itself, lifting and negotiating the few stairs between the cabin and Sean's truck. Eventually we did it and the bureau made it to my garage. I had William on that end to finish the job later and it was getting late, so, since we both had things to do, Sean and I said good-bye.

A few weeks went by. Sean called a couple of times to say hello and we talked very briefly each time. I considered driving to Silver Bay on a Monday night to attend the AA meeting that was his home group. I knew it was a bad idea - to be leaving on a school night and not getting back home until 8:30. Still, I went. Sean was not there.

On the drive back I had a committee meeting in my head. All the usual voices were there.

"*It's a good thing things worked out that way tonight. I mean, you do not want a boyfriend that is from your jail class. Remember what happened with*

Skeeter? And the thing is, Sean could be ... well who knows what? And how about this? You're twenty years older than Sean.

"Yeah, but Sean is a good person. I can sense that about him. He isn't devilish or a tease. He's right out there with his thoughts and his actions. There is integrity there and he is genuinely kind to me."

"Still, don't you wonder why he wasn't there tonight?"

"Well, not really, I mean things come up and who knows what other obligations he may have."

"Let it go. Assume it is a blessing. Let it go."

But no, I did not let it go. I had the disease of alcoholism whether I was drinking or not. Left unchecked, I twisted my own thoughts around until I convinced myself that what *I* wanted was God's will for me. Sean's gift of a cord of wood and his help with the bureau was just a hop, skip and a jump to, "*Hey, wouldn't it be fun to invite Sean to a concert in Duluth early in December?*" A longtime friend of mine, Peter Oshtrouska who played mandolin for many years on Garrison Keeler's radio show, "A Prairie Home Companion," was coming to a small church in Duluth to play a single free will donation concert on a Sunday night. Not a big deal, but a nice chance to go and hear some music ... with a guy friend. Well, a guy friend around which there were some jail rules and regs. A guy friend I could describe to my sponsor, which would be the right next step. I decided to sleep on it.

The next day I went ahead and invited Sean who said yes and quickly added that he would pick me up at 6:00 for the 7:00 o'clock concert. I made sleepover arrangements for William and Molly so I knew they would be happy with friends in town. The weekend began, I told no one; of course, I didn't call my sponsor and instead got ready to go out with Sean on Sunday night. I heard him pull up in the driveway, and so I walked out the front door to meet him.

There in my driveway was the car I had always referred to as a big penis for the compensating yet discriminating male - a classic Corvette - this one with some years on her, silver in color, sporting a few dings, but the real deal, a blast from the past. Sean, who was just getting out, got back in when he saw me which I took as my cue to walk to my side of the car, open my batman-type door and get in as well. I don't know how Sean did it, smoothly slipping into that car so low to the ground without the slightest struggle to find room for his long legs and torso. I felt like I barely fit, but no time to dwell on that. Sean revved the engine, and we flew down the dirt road at an ungodly speed, banking off the curves in the road to the "tune" of a silver bullet that had no muffler.

So much for those little nigglings, *"Is this really a good idea?"* We left them in the dust in the driveway. So much for not telling anyone what I was doing Sunday night. Inhabitants of the North Shore from North Star through the streets of Two Harbors to the East end of Duluth knew we were coming and if they bothered to look, may have recognized me.

Skip the time to talk on the drive. There was no point. There also was no music, just a lot of shifting, down shifting and engine revving until we roared into the church parking lot where Sean slammed on the brakes once he landed us in the nearest parking space.

I had absolutely nothing to say. I was speechless. I knew no car banter. I wasn't sure what a compliment to Sean about the car or his driving would even resemble. So, I think I pointed to the door of the church where the concert was being held as I squeaked, "I believe that is where we go in."

Sean seemed unaffected by my demeanor, the lack of color in my face or the arthritic look in my hands from grasping the seat and the door handle for 25 miles. Grateful to have arrived safely, I entered the church first and found a place for us to sit, up in the balcony in our own row where we had a perfect view of Peter O.

My friend's music, his voice, his artistry and the sounds that came from his mandolin were magic. Sean put his left arm around me early in the concert and never moved it except to hug and lean closer to me throughout the night. I was so happy. I didn't see anyone I knew. I completely forgot about the ride and just melted really, into the strong arms of a man I liked, who smelled good and was happy to come to a concert and hold me.

I was sad to have it end not because I was dreading the ride home but because I didn't want to leave the happiness that filled my spirit that night; especially the void that was always there as a condition of being on my own. I missed having a husband, a lover, someone who was there for me, whose best part of the day was for us to be together. It was a loss I knew I carried; I just didn't visit it often because it made me sad. Tonight, there had been Sean, a concert and a date night to make it go away, but now that was drawing to a close.

Sean drove us home the same way he had driven us to the concert, but it seemed more tolerable probably because it was dark, and the shock factor was over. We drove up the dirt road that became our driveway, a little slower than I anticipated, maybe because there were no lights, and the road had its unexpected twists and turns. Anyway, about three quarters of the way up, where the road flattened out a bit, I put my hand on Sean's leg and said, "Sean, do you think we could stop here … and neck for a little while before I go in?"

To which Sean calmly replied, "Sure," while he turned off the engine. And then he turned toward me while we jockeyed for a position that was comfortable given the gear shift in the middle of the front seats. We found one, I guess, because for the next ten minutes I was in heaven with a great kisser. Sean's lips were soft. He gently came toward me, slowly letting the first sensation of our lips touching take all the time in the world. And from there our hands barely moved to different parts of our bodies. It was all about our faces, and lips and tongues and tasting kiss after kiss. Occasionally we came up for air, but mostly not, just finding a way to breathe when necessary. I was getting hot, and the car was steamy. I pulled back a bit and said I thought I should go in.

"I have a great idea for a Valentine's present for you," said Sean, not adding anything else like a thank-you for the concert. I responded in kind with nothing, no thank-you for driving and a wonderful evening. We sat there in the dark with Sean's words -- just a little something left dangling that a boyfriend would say.

Sean drove up the rest of the driveway. I got out, now used to the manners protocol that excluded opening and holding doors for ladies. Before I closed my door, I leaned in, and we said goodnight. I walk-glided to the front door of my cabin. *Mmmmm MMM! That was so perfect.*

I never saw Sean again. He never called. Valentine's Day passed. I knew no one to call or anyone in his family to inquire about his wellbeing, though I doubt I would have. Many months later I ran into my favorite parole officer, and I asked him if he knew anything about Sean and how he might be doing.

"Oh yes," he replied. "He died - some accident of some kind most likely due to alcoholism. That poor kid, he never really had a chance. Everyone in his family was an alcoholic, both parents, all his grandparents, uncles and aunts on both sides of his family, his brother - everybody was a drunk. Plus, he had that bad accident when he was logging. I mean they saved his life by putting a big metal plate in his skull, but it was a funny thing. No one knew why, but every now and again something caused some kind of electrical activity in his brain because of that plate - and he would just go crazy - a wild man - destroying everything in his path. Still, I really liked him. He was a sweet guy, tried to make it out, but frankly, he didn't have a chance."

"Well, thanks for telling me, "I said after swallowing hard. I fought back my tears. "I didn't know most of that. I had him in my class at the jail. And I liked him, too."

Joanne, my friend and colleague at the Duluth Superior Symphony Orchestra was the only person I ever told about Sean. Soon after Sean died, she made a tape of music she thought I would enjoy, in the middle of which was tucked the song, "Samson" sung by singer-songwriter Regina Spektor. After I listened to the tape for the first time, I hurried to find Joanne to say that "Samson" seemed like a song about Sean.

"It was," she said.

I said good-bye to Sean in my heart of hearts.

"You were my sweetest downfall. Thank you for stepping into my life. I loved you. Rest in Peace, sweet friend."

Chapter 22

The Journey within the Journey

The road to financial maturity has been the most difficult, most exhausting, most humbling, and longest expedition of my life. It has also been the most freeing and the most empowering. It began when I was a little girl and didn't become a peaceful and gratifying part of who I am today until I was 73. To put that in perspective, the stories in this book occurred 15 years earlier than today which tells you I was operating in a world of ignorance most of my adult life. It also is a good reminder that it's never too late to tackle the big one.

My earliest recollection is that I loved playing with money. My favorite Christmas present ever was a sturdy, slightly brighter than pea green, metal cash register that had individual round keys, a drawer that popped open with a ding when you made a sale, and a display rectangle on top that showed a dollar sign, a decimal point and numbers. It could hold real coins and a few bills. It was indestructible, and my most prized possession even though I was given the "next model up" a few Christmases later.

My idea of a great Saturday morning was to play "Store." After watching "Howdy Doody", "The Lone Ranger", and "Sky King," on our black and white Sylvania TV, I would ask Mom if I could take all kinds of food items from our kitchen cupboards to create the store. She always said yes, up until the time I thought it would be a good idea to take the labels off the cans so I could write the prices in big numbers with cent signs.

"Annie, I like the new look of the store this week," she began, when she strolled into the living room on her way upstairs to do housework. "No labels - isn't *that* interesting? How exactly do you know what is in the cans?"

"Well, I know by the shape, like tuna or tomato soup, and I can remember what is in there because the cans are different colors and the prices are different," I was glad to answer.

"Of course, I see," she smiled not pressing the obvious like what about other customers who didn't have the inside scoop. I loved that about my mom. She didn't go berserk. Given this situation she simply introduced "Surprise Dinners" until all the bare-naked canned goods were gone, cheerily explaining to my dad why some meals were heavy on two or three different kinds of canned fruit with no veggies in sight. Eventually Mom replenished our cupboards when, needless to say, there were some new rules for "Store."

Labels or no labels, I stacked all the canned goods and Jello boxes in pyramids on footstools, couch cushions and chairs in the living room, organizing them by food groups just like they were at Red Owl, our local grocery store. Despite the absence of a gourmet section, it would be a mistake to assume that my store was either boring or limited in its merchandise. It was not. Take corn, for example. We had creamed corn, kernels of yellow corn, kernels of white corn, Mexican corn, corn with pimentos, in addition to large- and-small sized cans of several of those varieties of corn. And that was just one veggie.

Three dining room table chairs lined up next to each other in the middle of the living room made up the checkout area complete with a pile of brown paper bags and the cash register. The only other thing I needed if I wasn't playing by myself, was my younger brother, Robby, or my best friend, Wendy, and a decision as to who would shop and who would ring. I liked being at the cash register best, checking prices, ringing and counting money.

Another thing I liked was the way Grandpa McMillan entertained us when we went out for dinner at Lee's Kitchen in Highland Village, sometimes with just Grandma and him, and sometimes with Mom and Dad. Either way, my younger brother Robby and I were expected to have good manners, to sit still, to speak up with a please or thank you to the waitress and talk nicely with the adults. To help us pass the time before our food arrived, Grandpa would reach into the pants pocket of his beautifully tailored suit and pull out a handful of shiny coins which he put on the placemat in front of me. I would count them and come up with a total. He would look duly impressed when he checked my arithmetic to find that I got the total right every time. No prizes, just the fun of solving a problem, impressing my grandpa and a sense of self satisfaction that I was good at arithmetic and counting coins.

Not too long after that, my parents introduced an allowance of 35 cents a week, instructing me to put 10 cents in my weekly offering envelope that I took to Sunday school and to save the rest. Then once a year, I gave what I had saved to UNICEF's "One Great Hour of Sharing."

Coincidentally, the tooth fairy's going rate was 35 cents per tooth, provided there was a polite letter with the tooth. I babysat for 35 cents an hour and I noticed that gas was 35 cents a gallon. I had a savings account at the First National Bank and a little bank book that stayed in my dresser drawer except when we occasionally went to the bank.

With regard to life on the home front, we all worked together as a family after dinner and on weekends to do the dishes, pick up our rooms and take care of our home and our yard. There was no discussion about money. Chores were not tied to my allowance. Therefore, I concluded that we worked together as a family, we gave offerings of money to help others, and pretty much everything cost or earned you 35 cents.

My first summer jobs were volunteer positions, as an arts and crafts day-camp counselor and then as a candy striper at St. Joseph's hospital. When I was 18, I went off to Lawrence University. My dad died in May of my freshman year, and the next thing I knew, Mom and I were marching into President Curtis Tarr's office the following September to explain the situation and ask for opportunities for me to work. It was all a blur and only made sense to be sitting there because Dad had always said,

"When you need something, go straight to the top. That's the person who has the power to make the decision or get you to the right person who can help you."

All I know is that Mom did the talking; and that Curtis Tarr was extremely tall in person with the perfect nose for his stature. He was handsome and had a beak that was thin and straight and bony on top. It was noticeable, I thought, in a good way, like,

"*Yes, that goes together. Yes, your nose does, in fact, fit the rest of you quite nicely.*"

After our visit, Curtis and his wife frequently hired me to babysit, and I somehow got a job working at Conkey's bookstore one block off campus. After I had started my new Conkey's job, I found myself in a new situation - out of the monthly spending money that Mom sent me. I took five dollars out of the cash register on three separate occasions. I didn't know that Mr. Thielen, the owner, probably figured me out, because I didn't know any more about cash registers and their function in a business than I did at age five. I had no idea registers were balanced at least once a day, and shortages could be traced to who was working at that time. I also have no idea now, how helping myself to money in the cash register was okay with me. I believe I would have described myself as an honest person and not a thief. Upon reflection, I think it was simple. I needed a little money and there it was, so I took it. A random act. I felt guilty. I didn't think I should keep doing it. After three times I stopped and switched to washing cars to earn money, not only so I wouldn't have to steal anymore from Conkey's but also because I had a big goal, and the occasional five dollars wasn't going to get me there. I was saving for a plane ticket to Dartmouth College to visit my boyfriend, Josh.

During my first three years as an undergraduate, I spent a lot of time at Dartmouth which, in turn, required a lot of car washing, the humble beginnings of a worthy profession as a cleaning woman that was to save my life thirty years later. Josh came to Lawrence, too, but only once. We wanted to get married and jumped at the chance when I was accepted at Dartmouth my senior year, as one of 70 women in the college's trial run with co-education. The year was 1969. We got married on September 13th in my backyard, and drove the wedding present from Josh's parents, a platinum Ford convertible to which we attached a U-Haul, heading across the country for our senior year as a married couple. We were both full-time students, supported by our parents who were paying for our college education. I expect they arranged with Lawrence and Dartmouth to deduct Room and Board fees so they could redirect that money to us for living expenses off campus. I honestly can't remember how we came by money to live, but I remember shopping, cooking and having our share of fondue parties. I did not work but was busy in my major, theater, studying film, taking dance classes, and directing one-act plays while Josh pursued his major in religion and rowed for the college. My Bachelor of Arts degree was from Lawrence which I received in early June, by waddling to the mailbox eight months pregnant. Josh, too, received his BA from Dartmouth, but without ceremony. Adventure called and we left the campus early with the rest of the crew team for the Henley Regatta in England where our son, Oliver Sundance was delivered by a mid-wife on 7/7/70, one week after the crew team was victorious.

Yale Law School was our next stop where Josh and I lived on $30.00 per week, given to us by his parents. I washed diapers in the tub, shopped once a week and spent every penny on food for us and our baby, Sundance. We qualified for student housing, had no car and walked everywhere. I made a rug for our one-bedroom apartment out of free carpet squares that I sewed together with heavy thread and a darning needle. Our curtains were made of macaroni noodles I strung, hung, and selectively painted in primary colors. They matched our furniture which consisted of painted wooden packing boxes for fruit discarded by the grocery store, repurposed in our lovely home so we had book and toy shelves, a tv stand, and footstool. We were hippies, without drugs and alcohol because we couldn't afford it, but the upside of that was that our wardrobes required no investment. My assessment of that chapter of our lives? This sucks. My hands are raw. We need more money.

Unhappy at Yale, we returned to Dartmouth for two years while Josh took a break from law school to fill a position as an associate dean of students. Life was much better.

One of us was earning a living, plus we had a lot more fun, sharing an old farmhouse we rented in Norwich, Vermont, with my brother, Robby, and his roommate who were undergraduates at Dartmouth. The Dean of the college, himself an Oxford student, introduced my husband to the idea of completing law school in England where he could pursue rowing and an additional degree in ethics, both important to Josh. I had no burning desire of my own at that point. I was truly content with the fun of being a young mother, happy to be on the adventure with my husband, proud of him and enthusiastic about his dreams.

Both Oxford and Cambridge Universities sent letters of acceptance, so Josh set about choosing the right college and boat club for himself: Cambridge. I will never forget arriving at Trinity College, the two of us with a suitcase, a backpack and a three-year-old, looking across the Great Court, the largest enclosed courtyard in all of Europe, as if we had been photoshopped into a time and place too magical to understand, too formal for twenty somethings in jeans, too awe-inspiring for words. We stood in silence until Josh said, "Well, I had better find out about my classes and where the boathouse is located," to which I nearly replied, but kept to myself, *"Hey, wait a minute, we're a family here, what about a place to live first?"* When I took a moment to think, I understood that Josh thought family matters belonged to me and that he wasn't trying to ditch us. Furthermore, I didn't want to be a whiner, so Sundance and I pursued a lead about a flat in Dryden House which was to be our new home. In no time Josh made friends on the crew team and we became a part of the international postgraduate community at Trinity College, a richly diverse collection of adults from all over the world who arrived with their young families eager to make friends and share meals. We "mums" met for tea with our young ones Monday through Friday at the university club where we could talk while the children played and had an early supper of sausages, chips, biscuits and tea with milk. Like most everyone in Cambridge, Josh and I rode bikes, and I shopped every day at the open-air market. A bike basket and a baby seat on my bike were the extent of our investments, allowing us to live inexpensively in an economy where the American dollar went a long way as England had not as yet joined the Common Market. We discovered we could afford to fly home to Minnesota every summer, live with our parents, work law clerk and cleaning jobs, and earn enough to support ourselves for another school year.

Life in idyllic Cambridge was life-changing for the positive. Coming face to face with world history beyond the borders of the United States, sparked my desire to read, to travel and to see more, which Sundance and I did on weekends when Josh was rowing. I'd rent a car and choose a castle as our destination which meant that there was a church nearby where I could do some brass rubbings. I was beyond happy crawling amongst the cloisters with my little boy and his best friend, a stuffed animal named Foxie, while telling him the stories of kings, queens and battles about which I had read in my pre-trip research. After teatime we would take our chances on finding a vacancy at a bed and breakfast. Having accomplished that, we would set out for a nearby pub where there was always good company with whom we could enjoy our favorite dinner, fish and chips.

I fell in love with England the more I walked through her villages, took the train to the theater in London, stood in awe of her castles and lived a "civilized" daily life where businesses opened at 9:00 in the morning, tea was at 4:00 and dinner at 7:00 - adults only, as children were already in bed. As many days as the weather permitted, I pedaled alongside Josh's crew practice on the Cam River with Sundance bouncing in the child-size bicycle seat calling, "Daddy," his yellow curls lifted by the wind. We lived at a gentler pace, never rushing anywhere, living simply with a sense of peace and abundance.

Yet, despite it all, there was an important contrast to life in America that increased in intensity and increased my longing for home. The contrast was not something uniquely English to which I objected, the contrast was about something that was missing, something foundational, something essential — like air, something I could not do without.

For the first time in my life, I was coming to understand freedom. American freedom. I had glimpses of my thoughts as they were forming but they were just a flicker, a light in the distance like Tinkerbell in Peter Pan, the first play I took Oliver Sundance to see in London. I knew the words freedom and liberty. I knew they were my birthright as an American. But they were concepts that were elusive and hard to appreciate until I experienced living without them. In my 25 years of living, I had rarely been told, "No, you can't." Never had I been told, "You are not allowed, not permitted to try."

On the contrary, I had been encouraged to try anything I wanted, to spread my wings, to dream big dreams and to know that they were as possible for me as anyone else as long as I took responsibility for them and was willing to overcome the hurdles that would present themselves. No problem. I enjoyed the challenges as much as the achievements on the paths I had pursued thus far. I was used to saying, "Bring it on!" The difficulties were what made it fun!

There is no question that I lost my footing when my father died. I had the wind knocked out of me, and I was only too happy to follow Josh's lead early in our life together. He was clear about what he wanted, and I was proud to stand beside him. But deep in me and not to be shaken was drive and excitement about what I was going to contribute with my life. I may not have known what that was, but I sure as hell expected an equal chance, respect, and cooperation when I was ready to step out. In England, being a female not born into the upper class meant there was no future for my kind of spirit. That was becoming clear. The preamble to the United States Constitution promised me more than that, and I was starting to understand the enormity of my good fortune, to be born an American. Small, even seemingly unimportant things happened that made me think.

I read Leon Uris's Trinity, the story of Ireland, the Catholic and Protestant wars and the IRA; and then found in David Jennens, a doctor in Cambridge and one of Josh's rowing coaches, a person eager to talk with me about the complexities of that period of history and the interwoven, passionate struggles for freedom.

I went on guided walking tours in London, spent days in the British Museum and became engrossed in Winston Churchill's life, World War II and the fight for freedom in the face of Communism.

When we traveled to Orio, Spain for a boatrace, an older man in a pub sat across from me at a little table and then intentionally spilled his beer so he could write in it, "We love USA JFK." Once he knew I saw it, he quickly erased it with his palm so the paramilitary standing nearby with their M-16s wouldn't arrest him.

I was escorted out of a posh club in London where I went to meet Josh. "Gentlemen only, Madam. Please wait outside."

I was the only woman at many teas and special dinners because I was Josh's wife. On one occasion, David Jennens invited me to join the Cambridge Trinity First and Third Boat Club for a special excursion, a day of travel through the English countryside with a surprise destination. Shortly after arriving at a magnificent castle in the early afternoon where we were the exclusive guests for a tour of the estate, we were escorted to the castle's banquet hall. Once seated at a long, rough-hewn wooden table, we were served an eight-course feast of the most delectable food and wines I had ever enjoyed. It was a magnificent day, one I shall never forget, one that came to be because of the kindness and generosity of Dr. Jennens. As we drove home in the dusk of the early evening, I remember being silent, with feelings of gratitude for having been included at the same time that I felt apart from, a tag-a-long, an extra.

I was not allowed to see my husband for a month when Josh was training in London on the Thames for the Boat Race against Oxford. Even when the race was over, Sundance and I were ushered to the side and asked to wait when we tried to approach and congratulate Josh. I took it in stride at the time because it was part of English tradition, but I noticed more often than not that the position for women and children seemed to be one of exclusion.

I started to appreciate my country and the generations of people who fought for my freedom so I could have limitless opportunities. I realized I missed the sense of equal value as a human being that I felt in the U.S. I missed interest in and conversation about *my* thoughts, *my* interests, opportunities that intrigued *me*. Not happy and not knowing exactly what to do, I carried on with what I could do. I pursued my interest in theater, auditioning as an actor and stand-up comedienne in hopes of joining the Cambridge University Light Entertainment Society. When they added me to the company, I brought Sundance with me to all our daytime rehearsals and even some performances for children in orphanages, prisons and small community theaters. Never before was I as touched by an audience as by the children in an orphanage who loved my Princess character. They brought me to tears. Nor was I ever as misunderstood by an audience as by the drunken college boys who booed me off the stage at my debut as a stand-up comic. For too long, I kept going, dodging the soggy fruit from their Pimm's drinks, hurled at me at one in the morning. They brought me to tears, too, tears of relief when it was over.

More in keeping with the peaceful life of Cambridge, I pedaled to ballet classes three times a week. Keeping a low profile, I stood in the very back row of the class after settling Sundance near me in a corner with some books, hoping not to be noticed but rather allowed to attend and move to the music, just so I could try something I had always wanted to do. All in all, theater and dance helped immensely, but they never overcame the overall sense of being alone, second, and not so important. That was new for me, and I didn't like it. Fortunately, my glass-half-full orientation kept me focused on what we did have, the freedom and blessings to even be living in Cambridge, to break away from the pack, to make our own way. We three were a family learning to take responsibility for ourselves and how to care for each other. There were some imbalances, but generally speaking, we were a good team, and I was proud of us.

Unable to find a place to express my conflicting feelings and personal unrest, I turned to alcohol. Despite our outward success and the genuine friends we had made, I couldn't find the courage to speak to anyone, so I coped by taking advantage of sherry parties and pub life to quiet my anxiety as the disease of alcoholism was taking root in me. My history with alcohol was uninteresting at best, my first drink having been during my freshman year of college, in the dorm mother's apartment with my roommates. Daiquiris made with rum and little packets of powder tasted like lemonade, so I drank five waiting for something to happen. It did. I passed out. After that I drank when it was available and always to excess, passing out. I smoked two packs of Winston's a day and added bulimia to my bag of tricks while I was at Lawrence. During my pregnancy my senior year at Dartmouth, I cut out the smoking but continued to drink on weekends - always the same Lancer's rose wine - the perfect pairing for fondue parties. At Yale I didn't drink at all because adult beverages weren't in the budget. I know now that I was allergic to ethyl alcohol from the very start and on my way to life as an addict. But the progression was sneaky. I didn't see the erosion of my judgement and how addiction was taking over my life, mentally, physically, and spiritually.

Even I was shocked when I shoplifted a large piece of red-waxed Gouda cheese the size of a grapefruit, from Tesco's, a grocery store in Cambridge. Two policemen met me at the checkout, asked me to retrieve the cheese from under my coat before they arrested, handcuffed, and escorted me to a police car with Sundance in tow. After a trip to the police station for fingerprints, a mug shot, and brief discussion, one of Cambridgeshire's finest escorted us home and deposited me with my son on the doorstep of our flat on the third floor of Dryden House. Josh answered the door.

"Good evening, sir," the officer began as I stood there with Sundance, completely humiliated.

"I'm sorry to have to tell you that we just arrested your wife for shoplifting at Tesco's in City Centre."

"Is that true?" Josh asked, looking at me and Sundance in disbelief.

"Yes," I answered, thinking I'd give anything to have us all just drop through the floor.

Officially and like a gentleman, the officer jumped in to conclude the conversation. "Your wife will have to appear in court to plead her case. You may go with her to the courthouse which is also in City Centre. You will be mailed the details as to date and time. Good evening, sir."

A month later I went to court by myself where I stood before a magistrate in his white wig. I told the truth. Josh was in class, and it was my mess to clean up, so I was just as happy to be there on my own. I meant it when I told the magistrate I was sorry and that I was prepared to make it right in whatever way the court directed me. I don't remember the judge's exact words, but he spoke clearly, crisply, with perfect enunciation, adding only a few words of embellishment.

"Pay the court ten pounds and don't do it again," he concluded, his formality softening the blow but not erasing the very real awareness that I was lost and alone with a problem, that I didn't know what to do, and that it would be good to get back to the US where I could get my bearings. At the end of our three years in England, we happily returned to Minnesota bearing accomplishments: Josh's distinction as the first President of the Cambridge Blues, two Boat Race victories over Oxford, a law degree and an ethics degree; my show-stopping performances and contributions to the Cambridge arts scene, dozens of exquisite brass rubbings, and a fantastic chapter in our young lives as parents and a couple, despite the underlying problems that were not going away.

Returning to the United States was rough in the beginning. Despite our agreement that it would be my turn to go on to graduate school when we returned from England, Josh announced I would have to find work because we had too many law school bills. I was furious. But I hit the streets and was hired as a headhunter by the first employment agency from which I sought help. I was on a straight commission salary and made more money than my hotshot lawyer husband, at least for the first two years. I felt better. The third year I found myself a sweet job at Honeywell as a corporate trainer, where I rose through the ranks to lead a training organization of eighty with a ten-million-dollar budget. I didn't truly understand my financial responsibilities within the company, but I was eager to learn and was accountable for understanding the basics about budgeting, buzzwords like "P and L," "plan vs. actual," and "ROI." I was a skilled presenter and my organization's work was sound, so I successfully took my case up the organization where my proposals for growth were met with enthusiasm and the go-ahead for greater responsibilities and accompanying resources. For day-to-day management I delegated, surrounding myself with people whom I trusted, smarter than me and who did know how to wisely manage our finances.

With regard to me personally and how I was handling money, I obediently followed the directions of my financial advisor whom I trusted, a senior advisor named Kathrine at IDS Financial Services. We met for one half hour annually, and from there she proceeded to build my savings to three quarters of a million dollars over twenty years. I later learned there was a name for her strategy, "living below your means." I took home two thirds of my earnings while she worked with the other third.

There was one time in our first five years back in the US when Josh accepted an invitation to join the more senior partners of his law firm in their disciplines of building wealth. Josh told me about his Saturday morning plans to meet with the appointed financial advisor. I was interested and asked to go but was dismissed because it was just a gentlemen's lunch. Frustrated, I remained silent, caught somewhere between trusting my husband's wishes and my intuition that I should be there. I didn't like being excluded, that much I knew, though I missed the far more important point. By not attending, by not learning at ground level, I became irrelevant. In our prime earning years, as a power couple with two successful professions, I had lost an opportunity to be an informed partner in my marriage, and I lost my voice.

I remained a strong cash flow contributor but was a pain in the ass when it came to strategizing and decision making. So, *we* didn't do that. Josh did that by himself with the advice of the senior members of the firm. As a couple we never agreed to an overall plan for our lives and our resources. Josh had his track, I had mine, and neither of us checked with the other to see if we were headed in the same direction.

Two of us earning was different from the model I observed growing up in which my dad took care of my mom and our family through his earnings only. Josh and I were bringing in plenty of money, so I thought our life must be going well. Furthermore, I was proud that I was contributing to my family's earnings. I assumed that Josh would always put our family first, just like my dad had done. I assumed we had the same priorities and sense of responsibilities, which was unfair to both of us. We didn't. We thought differently. We spent our days in different worlds, identifying different kinds of problems and solutions, mastering completely different skills and strategies as we rose in our careers. I ran our household on what I brought home and asked Josh to write me a check at the end of the month if we had gone over, to which he always objected, but only for one minute. I could endure his displeasure and kept silent, naively curious as to why he objected, and yet not knowing what else to do. Looking back, I see that in ignorance we missed a huge opportunity to get to know each other as we learned new things, as our hopes and dreams changed, as opportunities for success presented themselves, and as we matured as individuals. Ultimately, we missed building a life together that I believe could have been a shared and truly satisfying achievement, not to mention a great love story of two kids who met in seventh grade.

Josh and I struggled as a couple. I got sober in 1981, we separated and got back together, had a beautiful second son, Christopher in 1983 and then sealed our desire to try our marriage again in a recommitment ceremony at our home with our two sons and fifty of our family and friends. I was excited about our new start and eager for therapy and what we would have to change to stay together. But what followed was five years of a rocky road.

When Christopher was six and Oliver was 18, Josh said, "I want a divorce."

I said, "I do not." But I could not make him stay. We took the next five years to complete that transaction.

During that time, I met Jack Stewart at an AA meeting. After a year of dating, Jack moved in with Christopher and me, and I found myself in another family configuration, two adults, unmarried, living day to day with my son, Christopher. I hadn't done that before, and I was uncomfortable. I couldn't resolve my mixed feelings about how I was choosing to live through a divorce, but I didn't try very hard either. I was tired of being left, of having my dreams shattered, of looking at an empty canvas for a future. I fell for Jack. I believed he loved me, and I knew for sure that being with him relieved the pain. I didn't care that I was supporting us. I had a secure profession, a lot of money, and a very generous child support check that came in each month. I rationalized the lopsided nature of our relationship (my house, my cars, my money) by convincing myself that Jack carried his share in other ways.

Jack and I had William in 1991. Then five years later in 1996, we had Molly, the same year I turned 50 and was laid off from Honeywell. Life was in full swing, and I was all in with a partner who liked to do things together and have fun with our children. In the ten years we lived together, I went from a positive savings of $750,000 to debt totaling $300,000. That's a million-dollar swing. I had no idea about the impact of the decisions I was making during that period of time. When I was surprised at the bills for our escapades, I flew into action to find the next source I could deplete to keep up with our lifestyle. Compared to the twenty years I had worked, I lost everything very quickly, in less than three years. I was in a hole, trying to dig myself out, unable to apply the simple wisdom of my AA sponsor, "When you are in a hole, stop digging."

I tried my best to keep our financial disaster from affecting Molly's and William's lives. Prior to Jack's exit and the great unraveling on the north shore, I did pretty well. But I know they felt it once we were on our own. They endured countless embarrassing moments like trying to pay for our Burger King dinner when we were twenty-seven cents short. They were in 3rd and 8th grades and fully present. Scurrying around to find some coins stuck in the seats or pockets of the car, we were unsuccessful and therefore, ultimately dismissed with a cheery, "Sorry, maybe next time."

The children watched me hand their dinner back through the window to the still cheery BK worker. The prickly silence in the car stayed with us as we pulled out of the drive-thru lane. It stung, not because we had a moment of coming up short, but because we were that close to the edge all the time, we all knew it on some level, and now here it was, alive and in technicolor.

Our situation didn't improve, and William took the reins at Gustavus Adolphus College to keep himself on track.

"Hi Mom, how's it going?" I would hear him begin the conversation we had at the beginning of each semester. William was working two jobs, and I was picking up the rest of his tuition and costs not covered by the mitt full of scholarships he had earned.

"Just thought I'd give you a heads up that tuition is due for the next semester. You should be receiving a letter."

"What do we need to come up with?" I'd ask. This was typical. I had promised I would get him through with less than ten thousand dollars' worth of debt, but I had no plan.

"You need to send in $3500 by next Friday." He would answer.

"Okay, I've got it," I would reply. "I'll take care of it. Thanks honey. How's everything else?" And then off the phone so I could call the business office to make some plan of partial payments.

Perhaps the worst thing I did for money, that I hid from William and Molly, was in the beginning when I cleaned houses at night after they had gone to sleep. It was the only option I could quickly implement in the first three months that we were on our own in the cabin. At bedtime around 8:30, I would lie down with them on either side of me on our side-by-side futon beds in the loft, holding their hands and dozing off myself for a few minutes. When I was sure they were asleep, I would slip out of their grasps and quietly climb down the ladder. Tip-toeing across the living room floor to the front door, I walked to my car in the driveway where I had packed my cleaning supplies for my drive to the cabin I planned to clean that night. Praying for all of our safety, crazy with anxiety as I scrubbed and vacuumed, I would clean no later than five in the morning, hurrying home to breathe a sigh of relief when I saw my children still asleep. I knew it was dangerous to leave them alone. I knew they might awaken and be terrified if they couldn't find me. I knew some freaky accident could take place. But, I had nothing else. The risks got to me though, and sooner rather than later. So I took the children with me on "adventure sleepovers" to fall asleep on other people's couches where I could keep my eye on them while I cleaned around them.

Looking back now at the financial trail I was leaving behind, I am struck with how many years I did the same thing. Everywhere I went I owed people money, sometimes a little, sometimes a lot. Except for the immediate expenses of gas and food, I never had enough to get fully current. I thought a good attitude coupled with a sincere desire to pay things off as quickly as possible was acceptable. In my mind that automatically gave me the right to go onto the next good idea for our family, despite the obvious fact to everyone but me, that we couldn't afford my choices and were living way beyond our means. One day I stopped at my new banking institution, the Credit Union in Duluth, where overdraft fees were less than those at Wells Fargo, hence, my decision to change banks. After the teller counted out the cash for my withdrawal she added, "Would you have an extra five minutes, Annie? Our Vice-President is in the office today and would like to talk with you. He's a very nice person and has an idea for you."

"Alright," I replied, a little nervous, but agreeable.

The door to the left of the row of tellers opened and Mr. Bank Vice-president appeared, "Hello Ms. McMillan. Please come in and make yourself comfortable."

As I sat down across from him at his desk, he continued, "I have noticed that you are spending a significant amount of money in overdraft fees every month and I wondered if I might help you with that. This last month, for example," he said as he referenced a document he had prepared, "your overdraft fees totaled $945 dollars and the month before they were at about $700. I am thinking that is money you could use for your family's expenses."

"Yes, it is," I agreed, thinking I did not want him to tell me to not write checks if I didn't have money in my account. I knew that already. But I listened attentively even though I had already done what he was going to tell me, "Build that cushion of a few hundred dollars." I didn't have the guts to tell him I had done that over and over again, but continued to find myself spending the cushion on what I deemed another necessity hoping that my latest cleaning check would clear the bank before the check I was writing. It was a mess and I had tried what he was suggesting. But, honestly, one good idea didn't have a chance. I needed a major overhaul.

Other good and kind, skilled professional people threw me lifelines, extending themselves as far as they possibly could to help. I made progress, but not really. So, I had a credit score that finally broke into the 500's. So, I was able to pay off some debt while staying within my budget. So, Janice, the hardest-working, most creative personal banker in all of Wells Fargo, who never gave up on me, thought I was going to come out on top... eventually. So what? The fact was I didn't come out on top or sideways, or any way on anything in the ten years Janice knew me because I had no idea how the whole world of personal finance worked! I could complete individual tasks, but they didn't relate to anything. As far as I could tell, I still owed a lot of people a lot of money so the best thing I could come up with was to work harder. If anyone offered me a job and it wasn't illegal, I pretty much said, "Yes," thinking it couldn't hurt. I had so much to learn and so little awareness of my ignorance. I just kept doing the same things while treading water to keep us from drowning. It was exhausting.

Ten years later I came to regret my "Just say Yes" philosophy when I was fired one morning as a barista only to be signed that afternoon as the mall Easter Bunny for two months. I guess my only relevant experience, as a child sitting on Santa's lap at the Southdale Mall and Dayton's Department store, was sufficient for Premier Events, my new employer. It was all about fun. It required patience and a good attitude, nothing too   strenuous, and so I suited up and prepared for hours in what turned out to be an inanimate sweat lodge. Imagine my surprise when I found out on my first Saturday as the Bunny that it was "Pet Day with the

Easter Bunny." I had no idea what that meant but took my job very seriously when two Doberman Pinchers found the bunny to be a real turn on. I was fighting for my life to get out from under at the same time I was recoiling from their tongues that were slobbering through my caricature eyes and mouth. I survived thanks to the photographer. I made some money and lost five pounds, but most importantly, I learned to complete a pro and con analysis of future job opportunities, an area of personal growth on my financial journey.

Two years after William left for Gustavus, Molly was given a full ride to attend the pre-professional Minnesota Youth Ballet Academy in Rochester, Minnesota. As soon as her eighth grade year ended, I drove her there to pursue her dream and then returned to Two Harbors where I sold the cabin back to the bank on a short sale, walking with zero. I rented a storage unit in Two Harbors for our stuff and drove back again to Rochester to catch up with Molly and start a new chapter, still having learned little about how to make prudent financial decisions.

Molly and the other ballet students were housed for the summer in a new, trendy downtown apartment building within walking distance of the Mayo Clinic. Without looking around at any other options, I rented a larger unit there, too, starting in September. Our neighbors were Mayo's resident physicians from all over the world, the best and the brightest, whose monthly rent was covered in their education plan. Not so for us. $2800 per month plus utilities took my breath away, but I thought I'd find that good job everyone told me I would, because it wasn't Two Harbors, for heaven's sakes.

That didn't happen. No one wanted to hire a 65-year-old. So, we moved two more times, settling into a home listed in the Minnesota Historical Register, located in Chatfield, 20 miles south of Rochester. It was the exquisite, red brick, 1890, four-story residence of the original town's bank president, and at $800 per month, a big improvement despite the daily commute and some heating challenges. It seemed like our general situation was improving because nothing was on fire, but my unaddressed debt was growing, and I had no plan. Along the way I also suffered the loss of Joy and Benny's friendship, after they helped us move to Rochester by driving their truck filled with our big furniture items. When Joy returned home, she decided to confront me and, in my opinion, had the gall to write me a scathing email about my dishonesty, signing contracts knowing I did not have the money to afford the payments. I never responded, furious that she dare tell me how to raise my children and what quality of life I needed to accept. Righteously angry, I remained in denial, continuing to throw problem solving and hard work at worsening situations.

Fast forward five years to my Tuesday night AA meeting in little church basement one block down the street from our home in Chatfield. I finally stopped running. Exhausted and desperate I broke down crying, "My life is a mess, financially and in other ways too. Nothing I am doing is working. I can never pay all my bills, and things are getting worse. My driver's license has been suspended for too many speeding tickets, I have debt that keeps growing, I'm working as a waitress and as kitchen help at two different restaurants, I have a daughter in her first year of college with new tuition payments I don't know how I will pay, and I need help."

When the student is ready, the teacher appears. How many times had I heard that? I also believed it. That night, this student was ready. I stopped digging. I was willing to do or not do anything to clean up the mess. And with that, the teachers appeared.

Walking out of the meeting that night, another alcoholic offered to tutor me to financial health. She was the CFO of her own family-run business, a pragmatic, kind, and gifted teacher with the ability to help me learn by breaking complicated concepts into building blocks with simple terms. She was calm and confident as she firmly offered direction, supporting me as I took first things first, and never letting more than a week go by between calls or a drop-in visit to see how I was doing. To this day we talk every week, and a great friendship has come of it.

Within that same month, I was given a scholarship to Dave Ramsey's Financial Peace course being offered at my church. I took Molly as my partner since it was designed for couples, figuring it was a good step for us if I was going to break the chain of financial ignorance I had passed to my older children.

As I began learning, I hit a new bottom. No longer running to keep up with my self-imposed work harder philosophy, I had time to see the craziness in the way we had lived and the total lack of knowledge I had provided my children as they prepared to make their way in the world. It was that about which I felt the absolute worst. It took some serious introspection regarding my behavior for over forty years, conversations with my sponsor and minister about my shortcomings, direct apologies to those I had harmed and a desire to make amends on the way to forgiving myself. Little by little, I came to a place of acceptance, and I made progress. I had a plan. I was accountable to myself and the other people who were at my side. I let the past go and marched forth toward a debt-free life.

The following year I took the same Financial Peace course again because I needed it. This time I asked one of the teachers, Kenneth, to be my mentor. When we met for the first time at his home to get to know each other and to set up my budget on the computer, I arrived with four brown paper grocery bags stuffed with all my financial information. Kenneth never batted an eye. Instead, he asked me to tell him a little bit about myself while he sat back and gave me his undivided attention for half an hour. At the end of my story, he said, "I am impressed that you have been able to handle such a difficult situation. It's usually the other way around, where a person goes from rags to riches, starting with nothing, but through determination, grit and tenacity, they build their capability and their fortune. But *you* went from having it all to losing it all, arriving at the bottom with a crash *and* without the knowledge of how to build, assuming you wanted to return to riches. And yet here you are. That is impressive."

"Thank you, Kenneth" I said, feeling a little less embarrassed about my portable brown bag office. "No one has ever said that to me before," I added as tears welled up in my eyes. "It feels good be acknowledged."

Kenneth is still my mentor. Since that day he has been at the end of the phone for questions, to listen to my thinking when I am in trouble or setting a new goal, to evaluate options at points of indecision, and to delight in all the debts I have retired. I never leave a conversation without his references to the teachings of the Bible and the spiritual principles that are the underpinnings of Dave Ramsey's work. I thank God for the chance to grow in an area of my life where I was blind, self-righteous, and stubborn.

In 2021, at age 73, I paid off my last debt. Having succeeded in putting Molly through school, I knew if I stuck with it, I could be debt free within another two years. I continued working three jobs until the Covid 19 hit. I lost my waitressing job, but continued nannying and cleaning houses until the day came, an ordinary Tuesday afternoon, when I phoned "Compassionate Finance" for the balance due and made the final payment. No fanfare, just a moment in March, followed by another moment when I wrote a big goose egg at the bottom my debt column. Zero never looked so good.

You might read that and think, "Was that really something to celebrate? What about the fact that you're sort of at the end of your life with not much time left to earn...73 and no money! That can't be good."

You would be correct. And I've heard that before. Instead of freaking out with impatience at the obvious, I continue to work the best plan I have been able to design, with help, of course. I cannot change *when* I learned how to manage my financial responsibilities. And, you would be right. I no longer have the advantage of time on my side where over the next thirty years, I can work a big job and build my savings to at least a million dollars. But I am sure that if I am in good spiritual condition with the God of my understanding, and work my plan, I will continue to figure out how to support myself and make a little extra to do some good.

What I know is this. I am abundantly wealthy and blessed to have more than my share of what it takes to be happy, joyous and free every day. I am grateful for that and hope I never forget that understanding. Building my fortune at this stage of the game is an awesome adventure - especially to be looking back at zero!

Chapter 23

Good Night

No matter where I go, I am Lake Superior's child. I am my mother's love of life. I am my father's grit. I am my children's imperfect guardian angel, my grandchildren's biggest fan. I am my Higher Power's perfect creation, on the job to watch for the next place I may contribute in thanks for the life I have been given.

I close this book with immense gratitude for the years William, Molly and I lived on the North Shore. I will never run out of memories that fill my heart with joy. Here are two of my favorites to say, "Good Night."

Molly

There was no better place to be than at the Duluth Convention Center's stage door two hours before opening night of "The Nutcracker Ballet" in which Molly, at age 12, danced the ingenue role of Clara. I watched her bounce up the steps with her ballet bag over her shoulder, while I gathered up the remains of her Erbert and Gerbert's tuna sandwich, reflecting on what a very special ballet season this was for Molly. The long-standing tradition at the Minnesota Ballet Company was that only one girl was chosen for the role of Clara and for only one year. Molly's ballet dream was to be Clara and now opening night was about to embrace her as a beautiful young dancer.

Around the corner a parking place waited for me where I could refresh my make-up before heading in early to find a seat somewhere in the middle of the front two or three rows. I always sat that close and as near to the middle of the auditorium on the night of Molly's first performances so I could see every bit of what she was creating. I wanted to feel her energy, and not struggle because there was some large person blocking my view. Admittedly, it was a bit close to the stage -- I had a full view of the orchestra pit -- but I didn't care because I would be back to take in all four shows of the run choosing a different seat for a new perspective at each performance. That night I was in heaven. I loved Tchaikovsky's score with Allen Fields' choreography, and my sweet Molly who danced from her heart.

From her earliest dance performances, tapping and lip syncing to "Singing in the Bathtub" to her last ballet performance twelve years later in front of her high school at an assembly, she lit up the stage. Parents, her teachers, directors and choreographers from all over the world, principals in the Minnesota Ballet company, in addition to hundreds of people I had never met, sought me out to say that Molly had a gift, that she brought them such joy, such delight watching *her* have so much fun dancing. I agreed. When Molly was dancing, she dropped into a world that was a perfect fit. From her strong, pointed feet to her equally strong and graceful fingertips plus every bit of her engaged ballerina body in-between, Molly was beyond happy to be doing what she loved - immersing herself in the music and movement, owning those moments when it was her turn to bring a ballet to life and give it away.

Molly seemed to grasp the honor and blessing that was inherent in being cast in a ballet role. She was intuitive, wise and focused beyond her young years. She showed up. She worked harder than anyone else. She performed what she was taught, bringing integrity and authenticity to the ballet itself and its director. She also knew she was powerful, and that magic happened when she was performing. Perhaps it was her animated facial expressions and her intentional engagement with the audience while she was telling her story through dance, or perhaps it was her smile, no matter what role or character she played, sneaking in to make an appearance. Whatever it was that connected the audience to Molly and she to them, it sent radiance and love into the hearts and lives of all who were present. She couldn't help it. It happened every time which was why I was so excited to experience that phenomenon whenever she took the stage.

I thought every now and again that I should take pictures of her or capture her performances on film like I saw other parents doing with their children, but I never did because I couldn't bear to take my eyes off her. It was a privilege to watch her, and to me, sacred, as I was drawn into the outward expression of God's presence in the daughter I loved. Now I am glad I sat there, completely in the moment, ready when the orchestra played its last note to jump to my feet as if shot from a cannon.

My children came to expect that I'd be first on my feet for a standing ovation until my hands could clap no more. If they were embarrassed, they got over it. Other parents and patrons of the arts undoubtedly concluded I had no discriminating taste. But that wasn't it at all. I meant it! Duluth was a great community, abundant with opportunities to study and perform in music, dance and theater. Moreover, Duluth was unique in that it was home to so many talented professionals who helped children learn and experience the joy of excellence as they shared something beautiful with their fellow artists and their audiences.

"Thank you!" I clapped, "Thank you to all of you who have given to our children! And thank you especially tonight for what you have given Molly."

William

William was a French horn enthusiast, not because he had always dreamed of playing the French horn but because of the all too familiar consequences of having a last name that started with a letter toward the end of the alphabet. In the first week of seventh grade William was excited about band and playing the saxophone. He already played piano and had his heart set on learning to play this new instrument. I was excited for him, too, because he picked up piano quickly. He was an impressive Guitar Hero player and sang in an elite youth choir in Duluth. There was no question that he had musical gifts, so I was anticipating that the mellow notes of a saxophone would be floating through our cabin soon.

"How did it go at band today and are we supposed to go out and buy or rent a saxophone?" I asked William as soon as I picked him up and was driving out of the school parking lot.

"I'm not playing the saxophone," William answered.

"Oh," I replied, surprised but expecting some different good news.

"The band teacher started at the beginning of the alphabet for last names, and we picked our instruments in that order."

"Oh, I see," I added, "So I take it all the saxophones were taken by the time she got to Stewart?"

"Yup," agreed William and not in a cheery way. " So were all the bass saxes, trumpets, coronets, clarinets, flutes and trombones."

"What was left? I'm dying to know," I asked with a little less enthusiasm.

"French horn. I hate the French horn. I do not want to play the French horn. I don't even want to try it." William stated, making his position on his first experience with middle school band, crystal clear.

"Yes, I get that," I agreed. "What a total bummer. Did your band director say anything else?"

"Yes," William answered as he started to wind it up. I could hear in his voice that he had had enough. "She said she was sorry I didn't get my first pick (make that *any* pick) but she knew I was smart and that the French horn was the most difficult and some say, the most beautiful instrument in all of the band; would I please try it for a couple of days and then come and talk to her about it? I said I would. I'm not going to like it."

Within the first semester, William was playing French horn with a small ensemble of professional musicians from the Duluth Superior Symphony Orchestra at small holiday gatherings in city libraries and other venues organized for caroling and the enjoyment of favorite Christmas melodies. Two years later William was playing in the St. Peter's High School band that won state competitions year after year, delighting Duluth communities with concerts that raised the roof and sent families into the night air humming tunes and back-slapping their children for a job well done.

The band concert I will never forget was not at St. Peter's, but during the month of July when William was a sophomore and one of the younger musicians accepted into a six-week long, summer intensive band program at University of Wisconsin in Superior, Wisconsin. Their final week had been a scorcher with no change in temp and humidity as the Friday night event approached. This was the Showcase Concert, billed as the concert to end all concerts, and at six o'clock it was 105 degrees with no wind or even a slight breeze.

Nevertheless, enthusiastic parents, having paid a pretty penny for the privilege of driving their kids from miles around to and from camp every day, all showed up with more family members and squeezed into a small church type building that despite having a second-floor balcony, was standing room only. Once in the door nobody dared leave and give up their spot which didn't help the situation. We all stayed put, generating more heat waiting for the concert to begin and then listening to concert selections that were impressively difficult and beautifully played, but, honestly, just not good enough to compel you to stay in the God-awful heat. I was drenched with sweat and breathing heavily in the last row of the balcony while Molly, weak from the heat, slumped against me. Then, just when I had told myself, this was going to have to be the last piece we could endure, it *was* the last piece and, as it turned out, well worth every bit of discomfort that night.

I recognized it immediately as "Pirates of the Caribbean" with its rat-a-tat- tat snare drum that accompanied Johnny Depp's Captain Jack Sparrow approaching dry land and smoothly stepping onto the dock. From there the music became the sea, with small waves of the theme rolling in and then a musical bridge to a new key, building to increasingly larger, billowy waves of music that tumbled and folded into each other until five minutes later every instrument was being blown at full volume by lips on faces that were as bright red as candy apples. I thought the director would never quit. And then, with the final downstroke of his arm, the place erupted with raucous cheers and applause for an incredible voyage on the Caribbean, complete with sweat and salt water of our own making.

Despite the intense desire to hurry home and strip down to bare-naked, which was what everyone from the concert was thinking, William, Molly and I took time to engage with kids who were yelling, "Hey! Congratulations William!" "Way to go champ!"

"Congratulations on DDR, William. You were awesome!"

William said very little to his bandmates other than, "Thanks. Great concert tonight. See you next summer," while I piped in with, "The concert was great tonight, you guys. Thank you so much for a spectacular evening."

As we finished our walk to the car, I recalled that William had mentioned a Dance Dance Revolution contest and that it was a big tradition at the camp. What I didn't hear or pay attention to was that the same guy who had won it for the past five years was back and rumored to be unbeatable. And I definitely didn't pick up on the fact that the highly competitive, reigning defender of his title was none other than the band director himself.

Mr. Band Director looked like Humpty Dumpty, a person you could describe as round, and nobody would argue with you. He had a pretty face with great coloring, perpetual rosy cheeks and a shaved head for a clean, put together look, albeit without much variety - madras shirts, tan khaki pants, dock siders, and a handsome belt that was selected for utility in addition to completing the outfit. Mr. Band Director seemed like a lot of fun. Based on the performance he had gotten out of the kids that night, I imagined he was also a demanding teacher who drove his high standards home day in and day out. I could see him as a formidable competitor. Apparently details about challenging him as champ of Dance Dance Revolution made their way to William in the form of warnings from older kids.

"Mr. Band Director *runs* this place!"

"Yeah, I don't know what he would do if he lost!"

"He's kind of a maniac about it!"

That didn't deter William from going after something that he knew he could do, which in this instance was beat the pants off of Mr. BD. And that's exactly what he did.

"Oh my gosh, William!" I laughed as I caught on to what the congratulations were all about. "When did all this happen?"

"*I* know when it happened because I watched you practicing in the living room," piped in Molly.

"Is that right?" I continued incredulously, "You just practiced at home and then won? What was that like? When was the contest? What did your band director say?

"Yup, it was fun," said William, "This week after lunch all the challengers danced against each other until everyone was eliminated but me. That took three days and then yesterday I was up against the champ. I don't think he thought I would ever beat him, but I did, and it was great. Everyone cheered and he was decent about congratulating me. So, I'm the new champ."

"Amazing," I smiled, "Well, we sure got our money's worth out of this gig."

We drove home in laughter with the air conditioning on high, stopping for Dairy Queens that melted faster than we could eat them, thanking William for an incredible evening, a night we would never forget.

And that's how life was with William. He was generally the younger one keeping up with the pack until he figured out how to lead the pack, excelling in some extraordinary way that surprised the heck out of Molly and me...and many others.

"Ah William, yes William," his teachers would invariably begin their parent-teacher conferences, smiling with anticipation at telling me about what had never happened in the history of their teaching lives until they met William. From there they would spend about ten seconds showing me their master grading sheet, quickly pushing it aside once I saw all the boxes filled in with 100 percent or close to it. And then they would launch into their descriptions of the conversations with William that they personally found engaging and stimulating, describing his ability to digest and integrate large amounts of new material, seeing three steps ahead to outcomes and possibilities, and asking questions they had never considered.

What warmed my heart as William's mother was seeing his high school embrace a leader who wasn't a jock, who liked learning, who helped others, who volunteered to raise money by calling alumni and who tried out for the musical, "Brigadoon" as a sophomore, for God's sake, just because the director didn't have enough men in kilts. If William could make something better, he did. His musical solo selling sausage in "Brigadoon's" first act was enough to make you slump in your seat with embarrassment for him, which I would have, had he not commanded the stage with such aplomb. I sat up as did other audience members around me.

"That kid's got something!" I heard, followed by, "Who is *he*? I haven't seen *him* in any of our musicals before."

Like I always told my children, "There are no small parts, only small actors."

William made life at St. Peter's fun for everyone by engaging others with humor and humility which attracted friendship and admiration from the staff in the office, the custodians, his teachers, other parents and his community of fellow students. In chemistry, art and music, William's teachers described demonstrations of unusual curiosity, tenacity and productivity which, for example, resulted in one entire five shelf drying rack in the art room for William's pottery; positioned next to one identical drying rack for the rest of the class.

While the other band members stayed after school to practice their minimum 20 minutes, William practiced for two hours. In the chemistry lab, William was putting in many times more than anyone else because he was introduced to a field that interested him. And it kept on interesting him through his Ph.D. with which he began his professional life. At the same time, he discovered an interest in law and patents, so he did the course work and passed the exam for patent law.

Living with William was like walking on the surface of the earth in the land of the buried treasure. As a fellow traveler, the adventure was watching what

William noticed and then burrowed to the center of the earth to fully understand it. I got used to preparing to be amazed. It was humbling. I loved that his teachers described him as a scholar, a natural leader, a beautiful young man with great compassion, an unusually bright and talented human, and a really good person. That's the boy I knew, too.

Now, you tell me how I could see these years of my life as anything other than a huge blessing.

One truly exquisite place to live - where no matter which direction I looked, it took my breath away.

Two beautiful children with talents to discover, the courage to overcome excruciating loss, and goodness in their hearts to relish and then pass along to the next.

Immeasurable freedom to figure out how best to live as children of God, in gratitude, in service, in joy.

Time to grow up, to take responsibility for ourselves, to own our lives, our failures and our victories.

I smile when I remember our escapades and adventures. Our life on the North Shore sustains me when I'm blue, and it makes me laugh out loud when I least expect it.

I hope our stories have the same effect on you, inspiring you to keep going if life is difficult, finding ways to give generously no matter how life is treating you.

"Step out in faith and expect God to help," I was taught. "No matter what, step out!" I would add.

I have imagined this book on your bedside table, offering comfort, encouragement and a moment of peace at the end of the day. Perhaps it has found its way there. I hope so. Until we meet, I wish you love and laughter, and an abundance of blessings.

Made in the USA
Monee, IL
30 May 2024